BACK TO SCHOOL
SURVIVAL
MANUAL

BACK TO SCHOOL
SURVIVAL
MANUAL

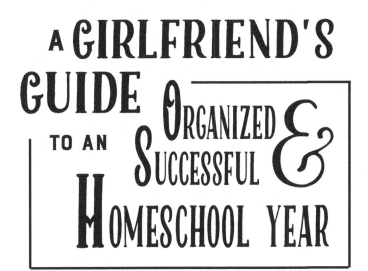

A GIRLFRIEND'S
GUIDE Organized &
TO AN Successful
Homeschool Year

ALICIA MICHELLE

ISBN-13: 978-1517109462

ISBN-10: 1517109469

Publishing and Design Services by MelindaMartin.me

CONTENTS

ACKNOWLEDGMENTS

To the women of the Vibrant Homeschooling community, and my fellow home-schooling bloggers: You are beautiful, unique, and it's my privilege to share this homeschooling journey with you. Thank you for your friendship.

To my Mom and Dad: Thank you for raising me, and for all the back to schools you saw me through. Dad, you've always believed in my writing, and as a child, you told me over and over that I could be anything that I wanted to be. Those words meant so much then, and they still mean a lot to me. Mom, thank you for always listening to me, especially on those days when I am tired and exhausted from this thing called parenting. You've reminded me many times that it will all be OK (and you were right). I love you.

To my four extraordinary children: You are each amazing, beautiful creations of God and I sometimes sit back in awe (and more than a little fear) that your dad and I get the privilege of spending these years with you shaping you towards your individual destinies. Be brave, be bold and be the wonderfully passionate souls you were made to be. Live your life without any regrets. And most of all, live your life all for Him. I love you and will always, always be here to cheer you on.

To my loving, amazing husband: How wonderful it is to be married almost 15 years and to know that you're falling more and more in love with your spouse every day. I don't know how I would live this life without you. Thank you for being my confidante, my cheerleader, and the finder of my lost things. You are one of the best gifts God has ever given me. I love you, my precious one.

To my God and my savior: If there's anything good in me, I know without a doubt that it's because of you. You have created every facet of me, and each day you sustain me to complete your calling for me (in my own imperfect way). I am humbled by your inexplicable grace, your unending love and your immutable plan for my life. In you and with you, my soul finds rest and purpose. You are my everything, and I love you.

To the Master Teacher who invented the idea of new beginnings and fresh starts.

INTRODUCTION

S o here you are, face-to-face with another school year. Perhaps this is your first year as a homeschooler (if so, congrats and welcome to the adventure!). If you've homeschooled before, I say to you too: Welcome to the adventure!

Do you get my point?

Every homeschool year (yes, every single one) is an adventure. Regardless of which "perfect" curriculum or learning method we choose, homeschooling is *never* a clear-cut, easy journey, and things *always* turn out differently than we expect.

There will be huge learning curves—for you and your kids—as you embrace new concepts and encounter new parenting stages. And those learning curves can really throw you for a loop (and if you've yet to experience that, you can just take my word for it).

The unexpected can happen and often does.

Can we just welcome and accept that now? Trust me, I'm preaching to my own self as I type this.

It's like taking a cross-country family road trip: You have a pretty good idea of where you'll end up on the trip, but honestly, **you set out on the journey not knowing what detours or adventures will happen along the way to your destination.**

Like having your tire blow out (on the freeway, in a not-so-nice part of Albuquerque) at midnight after driving for fourteen hours straight with a van full of kids and moving boxes.

Like having to stay an extra three days in Albuquerque (which was *not* your intended destination) while a local tire shop searches across a three-state-area for a tire that fits your van's custom rims (that you didn't know you had).

Like having to file a police report on your tire's blowout because it was caused by road traffic signs that had blown unexpectedly into the fast lane of the freeway.

Not what I expected when I signed up to help my in-laws move to Texas a few years ago.

But, oh… it *so* exemplifies what the journey of a homeschool year can look like.

Why are we talking about this? **Because the best way to be ready for the unexpected is to be prepared for the unexpected.**

Not in a creating-a-master-schedule-for-every-hour-from-now-until-June kind of way. (Laugh if you will, but that was me when I first started out, and you can read all about it in my first book *Plan to Be Flexible*).

Instead, I'm talking about **having a realistic and wise set of methods and thought-processes to serve as a strong foundation for the learning year ahead.** A systematic way of looking at the year and readying yourself—and your homeschool—for it.

That's what this book is about.

The Back to School Survival Guide's purpose is to be a tool to help you develop core strategies and systems to successfully set up your homeschool.

Meant to be a coaching tool with forms to be re-used year after year, the book outlines basic systems and thoughts for getting started off on the right foot.

And like all the books I write or courses I teach, my goal is to help you feel like we're just hanging out together over coffee, talking one-on-one together through these topics.

I want you to finish this book feeling refreshed, excited and *confident* about the school year ahead.

Even a school year that's potentially fraught with a few "midnight-tire-blow-out" experiences.

Because, let me tell you, even though they are often painful to endure, these moments are often the greatest times of growth and stretching for a family.

Let's give our homeschool the strongest foundation possible—one ready for whatever comes our way.

You can do this! I can do this! Let's get started on this back-to-school journey together.

With hope, excitement (and a spare tire in my trunk),

Alicia

P.S. You'll find something called the "Back to School Checklist" in the "Activities & Printables" section in the back of this book. I encourage you to use this resource as you move through each section of the book, checking off each item as you move through the process.

For your convenience, the complete Index has been
made available to you for ease of printing

http://bit.ly/1PYo2Eg

You will need the following password to access this document:

BackToSchool1234

You can also access all of the resources that I have referenced in this book at

http://wp.me/P4R9E2-1LK

PART 1: LAYING A FIRM FOUNDATION

CHAPTER 1: MAMA, THIS IS YOUR SCHOOL (AND NO ONE ELSE'S)!

Before we begin a discussion on some best practices for organizing and structuring your homeschool for back to school, I want to make one thing perfectly clear: **This is *your* homeschool, not mine.** You are the one who calls the shots. You are the one who makes the final decisions about how you will set things up, and how your school will run.

No one else.

Perhaps that seems like a obvious—and even unnecessary—statement. Of course we're in charge of our own schools! Of course we're the ones who get to make the final call about how to raise our children!

We may believe this, but truth be told, some of us aren't living this way.

I see homeschoolers—smart, creative, capable women!—all around me **who are truly *paralyzed*.** These are women who **seemed to know how they wanted to structure their homeschool, but have had their confidence shattered by an overwhelming flood of input from others.**

They find themselves stuck in a sea of thoughts, opinions and "advice"—many of it being the unsolicited kind. While admittedly some of the ideas have been helpful, the **sheer number of ideas and thoughts continually bombarding their mind uproots their confidence and leaves them floating aimlessly from wave to wave.**

I'm all for gathering new ideas and learning from others (and I'm guessing you feel the same way since you're reading this book), but I admit that I find myself in this "paralyzation of ideas" camp all too often.

And so, on a regular basis (and especially when I begin a specific quest to learn about a new aspect of my homeschooling), I need to remind myself that **my husband and I are the ones in charge of this homeschool venture.**

And ultimately, since my husband and I are Christians, we trust God to lead our homeschooling efforts, and so therefore, all answers about what is "right" and "wrong" for our family in this season come from the leading of His Spirit.

I'm bringing this up now because I want you to walk into the school year *confidently.* I want you to be able to see the areas where an over-abundance of ideas may be more harmful than good in building your solid homeschooling foundation.

I want you to be able to identify in yourself those things that cloud your vision for what your school year needs to be about *right now.*

Because—let me make this perfectly clear—your school is going to look different from mine; and not only is that OK, but it is natural and *good.*

Therefore, let's take this chapter to identify some of the sources of this influx of ideas and opinions; and **let's begin strategizing ways to regain that confidence required** to walk boldly into this school year's plan and purpose.

3 MAIN SOURCES OF OUTSIDE OPINIONS

1. Social Media

I am a huge, huge fan of social media. Although it definitely has its shortcomings (which I'll get to in a minute), the opportunity to connect with others from all over the globe through a few key strokes on a computer or taps on a hand-held device is truly extraordinary!

As a blogger, social media is also a critical tool for me. I am on Twitter, Facebook, Instagram and Pinterest (ahhh… *Pinterest…*) all day long: catching up with family and friends; engaging in conversation with readers and other bloggers; … **and filling my mind with a never-ending stream of new ideas.**

Which is where the trouble with social media starts to play out.

New ideas are great. They're fantastic. They can be like a tall glass of lemonade on a hot summer day—helping us to solve a problem that previously seemed insurmountable;

encouraging our hearts to stay the course when we are weary; and inspiring us to try new and exciting concepts that we may never have thought of on our own.

Or, ideas can be the spark for something that we humans are all too familiar with: the beast of comparison.

We *were* content with the decorations in our living room… until we went on Pinterest and saw *that couch* with *those pillows* and *that throw rug.*

We *did* think that buying a box of pre-made brownie mix was alright… until we saw *that homemade recipe* for triple-layer chocolate fudge walnut brownies with a peanut-butter-cup ganache.

And we *did think* things were OK with the way we educated our children… until we read *that post* about the "best" way to teach or the "best" way to run a homeschool day.

In fact, sometimes all these great ideas can do more harm than good. Instead of a blessing, social media's onslaught of ideas can become fodder for the comparison beast.

It's all so subtle, isn't it? **And it's this subtlety (and slow layering) of the messages that is our ultimate downfall when it comes to dealing with comparison.**

Also, the thing with ideas—at least ideas presented on social media—is that **they seem to find us without us looking for them.**

Everywhere you look on social media, **someone has an opinion about something.** Everyone seems to have a solution that will meet a need (and they're more than happy to share about it, whether we'd like to hear it or not).

My point is that, after a while, **all of these ideas—good or bad, and solicited or unsolicited—fill our hearts with a certain amount of discontent.**

Granted, we may find answers to some of our dilemmas, but because of the sheer quantity of opinions, thoughts and viewpoints continually floating around, social media by nature lends itself to the paralyzation that we previously mentioned.

2. Other Homeschoolers

It all seems innocent enough: We talk openly, as moms do, and we share homeschooling ideas and the latest news about our kids.

We would never admit that we are in competition with our fellow homeschoolers. And I truly believe that we don't *intend* to be this way.

But sometimes it's there in the eyes. If we look with a discerning spirit, we can see that tension… that longing in our friend's face (or we can feel it in our own heart).

It's that feeling of "wow, I could never do that": A simple statement that begins to slowly gnaw away at our self-esteem, our value and our mothering efforts.

And with a certain look, a shrug, or a too-bright smile as a response, we begin to exhibit these ugliest of emotions between sisters: envy, jealousy and comparison.

Of course we would never admit this to each other. We only access these bitter places in the most honest of moments. **Those times when we finally can see that we've been making unrealistic demands of ourselves, and we are digging to discover the "why" behind them.**

It's in these moments when we ask ourselves, "What am I doing? Why do I think that I must do these certain things my friend is doing in order to be a good homeschooler?"

That's when we can finally see the **despicable weed of** comparison **that's bloomed between us:** the ugly shrub that now horribly skews our perception of what makes the homeschooling life "bad" or "good." **And we realize that we've judged ourselves (and others) in the name of what we believe to be the "correct" answer to that question.**

Even worse, we realize that this toxic process has reduced our mom relationships to a comparison game where we've placed ourselves on a pedestal side-by-side: one party being "right," and the other being "wrong." Which, sadly, **reduces our friendships to a checklist of who's-doing-what-better.**

3. Well-Intending Nay-Sayers

You've heard the comments. You know the conversations.

In fact, because they seem to almost follow a predictable pattern ("What about socialization?" "What makes you think you're skilled to be a teacher?" etc). Answering what I call the typical homeschool "naysayer questions" seems almost comical after a while.

And yet, they can still shake any homeschooler's self-confidence. That's because, as humans, anytime someone questions us on any topic—no matter how valid our argument or true our answer is—that little tiny question of "what if?" can be deposited in our soul.

And of course, when those conversations involve a family member or close friend, they are way more impactful to our psyche because we value and respect their opinion.

How do we deal with this? We will address this in more detail in Chapter 2 when we talk about establishing your "why" as a foundation for your homeschool.

But, for now, I want to say: First, it is normal (and human) to be impacted by other's nay-saying opinions and that these negative questions can shake our self-confidence.

THE PLAN TO REGAIN CONTROL AND MAINTAIN SELF-CONFIDENCE

As I stated in the beginning of this book, I want to not only give you the physical tools to get your school started on the right foot, but I want to give you the mental tools as well.

And maintaining confidence in your homeschooling plans for this season is one of those big issues that must be addressed.

There are a few simple strategies I want to suggest here. Some of them may seem obvious; and others might be brand-new to you.

1. Turn Down the Noise of the Naysayers.

All that input you're receiving? **I'm not suggesting that you remove it completely, but simply *turn it down*.**

For social media, **maybe that means removing yourself from certain Facebook groups or "unfriending" a few people whose thoughts or ideas aren't supportive of your homeschooling philosophies.** These people may or may not be necessarily anti-homeschooling; in fact, they just may offer opinions on learning styles that are different from yours.

Or maybe they have *too many* good ideas and that's overwhelming! I can think of one specific homeschooling blogger's newsletter that I unsubscribed from, not because her ideas were contrary to how we were homeschooling in this season, **but because she had *so many* of them that I found myself constantly chasing the wind of her good ideas** instead of staying true to the teaching method I'd planned (which honestly, was working just fine).

Honestly, it can be really difficult to "turn down the noise" of those naysayers who are friends or family because many of those are permanent relationships and therefore there will be numerous opportunities to interact (and to potentially hear unwanted advice or comments).

I believe that the best strategy here is to simply develop your "why" and to politely but firmly stand strong in it. More on that in Chapter 2.

2. Reframe the Comparison Into Inspiration.

I'm convinced that **we all struggle with** the beast of comparison because we were created with a need to relate to each other. This is a survival instinct of sorts—a way to look at others for ideas in dealing with common issues.

However, through the lens of a sinful heart (which all of us have), this "need to relate" quickly twists into a lust for what is not ours; a heart of ingratitude for a situation that is "better"; and an overall discontent with our own life circumstances.

Instead of competition, what if we instead looked at each other as mirrors: me able to see inside your soul and to relate; and you to be able to see and relate to me as well?

This is inspiration (not comparison). Instead of a twisted, unspoken dialog of "they're better at this than I am, and therefore, I am bad," inspiration is what I believe God intends for us to develop in community.

What if we were able to re-frame that "good thing" we see happening in someone else into inspiration for a great idea for ourselves?

And, on the flip side, **can we be confident enough in our own calling so that we can say "that idea is a great one, but it's not for our family in this season" without the baggage of their idea being "good" and ours being "less than"?**

I believe it all comes down to an ultimate understanding of this simple statement: My homeschooling journey is my own, and your homeschooling journey is your own.

Let that sink in. How could that one concept revolutionize how you relate to others and others' opinions? I have to remember this thought *regularly* in order to translate comparison into inspiration in my heart.

When we can understand—and respect—this concept, new worlds open up for us! Once we have our true north (and can respect the "true north" of others), **we can begin filtering out what is good and helpful in this homeschool season and we can confidently walk in** our plan.

It all starts with defining your true north (which I refer to as your "why"). And that's exactly what the next chapter is about.

Points to Ponder

• How have you seen the outside opinions of others (even positive opinions) shake your homeschooling confidence?

• In which areas (social media, other homeschoolers or nay-sayers) do you see the greatest influence from others in your life?

• After reading this chapter, do you feel that you should begin placing limits or filters on how you allow these influencers into your life? If so, list the specific areas and some ideas to change.

For Additional Info

• Mom Competition: Can We Stop the Madness?

• "…but am I doing enough school?": Homeschooling Through the Tough Seasons

• When Homeschooling Is Lonely and Hard: An Honest Conversation from One Mom to Another

Helpful Resources

• "bloom: A Journey to Joy (and Sanity) for Homeschool Moms" Online Video Course

Related Activities and Printables in This Book

• Back to School Checklist

CHAPTER 2: WHY ARE YOU DOING THIS, ANYWAY?

Now that we've given you the freedom to develop the type of school environment that you think is best (without feeling the need to chase others ideas or be swayed by those who seem to have a "better" opinion), let's talk about the other side of that coin: What do you want your homeschool to be about? What type of ideologies or teaching styles do you want present?

In short, why are you doing this, and what does it look like for your family?

I truly believe you need to have this answer clearly defined before *every* homeschool year. Why?

Because, to be completely honest, your confidence level will be shaken. People *will* give you a hard time about some aspect of your homeschool decision.

Also, every year is different, which means that your homeschooling's focus may shift. Some years your family will be under unique levels of stress (for us, that was two years ago when we bought/sold a home).

Other years you'll need to adjust your priorities (and thus your expected daily activities) because you may need to prep a child for college or to lighten your load so you can care for a new baby.

And, perhaps most importantly, there *will* be days when you will just want to flat out quit.

WHEN IT'S TIME TO QUESTION EVERYTHING

Last year we endured one of those critical seasons. Our then-twelve-year-old was going through some difficult emotional issues and every day our homeschool was an absolute battleground.

We knew that somehow things had dramatically shifted for him. The daily structure of our learning environment was no longer working. It was difficult to describe, but we could tell that, without a doubt, **homeschooling as we'd been defining it was no longer a good fit for him.**

He had a dichotomous need to have both intense, one-on-one teaching time with me (which was nearly impossible with three other children to homeschool!); and also a great need to learn from other adults.

He was no longer thriving and desperately needed something to change.

This was shocking to us, and honestly, the last thing we'd expected. Wasn't homeschooling the best option for all of our kids? We'd never encountered this situation before and, honestly, never thought it would come up—especially for this special needs child for whom homeschooling had been a godsend.

And yet, last November **we found ourselves placing every schooling option on the table in front of us.** We looked at local private and public schools, considering not just the educational quality of each option, but our son's clear need for new social outlets and special needs services.

It was a gut-wrenching, grueling time bathed in many tears and countless prayers.

Finally, we felt led to a unique schooling option that allowed our son to be in a traditional school environment two days a week (with other homeschooled children) and learning at home the other three days. This school also offered special needs programs that would help with some of the additional social skills training he required.

There was room for our other children at this school as well, and this was an essential piece of the puzzle too because their at-home education was suffering because of my son's all-encompassing needs and ongoing emotional outbursts. The best part? They could attend the school on opposite days of my son. Although this meant I was driving back-and-forth to a school four days a week (again, something I never ever expected to do!), having my son on an opposite schedule from the other children enabled me to have two full days a week where I could spend concentrated time helping him through his most challenging subjects.

My point in telling you this story is to encourage you to determine your ultimate purpose for your schooling, and overall, for guiding your children as their parents.

During this season, we had to ask ourselves some tough questions about why we were doing this homeschool thing. **And we discovered that our "why" behind homeschooling was really rooted in one of our key parenting goals: To give our children the best learning environment for their individual needs during each life stage.**

Up until that point, traditional homeschooling had been the vehicle to meet that goal. But after this experience, we discovered that nothing was too sacred—including our love of homeschooling—if it meant that one of our children was suffering.

Developing your "why" is the critical element that will power you through the tough times. It will also serve as a plumb-line for determining which activities or studies are beneficial.

In short, your "why" serves as a blueprint for how to outline your days, and it also fuels you with the confidence needed to complete those days. That's why I say (before you buy curriculums and follow a teaching methodology), do some soul-searching and get to the root of your "why."

I would suggest that you not only develop an overall "why" behind your homeschooling, but a "why" that applies just to this year.

START BY ASKING "WHY NOT?"

My guess is that if you have made the decision to homeschool, you've probably thought through (at least partially) the "whys" behind the decision.

But have you worked through the "why nots"?

When my husband and I were able to work through our own fears and concerns about homeschooling (and truly address the opinions/pressures we may have felt from society, friends or family), we discovered so much freedom and joy!

That's because we knew we'd fully examined every aspect of the issue and could one hundred percent say that yes, we were on board for this year's journey.

It doesn't mean that we're arrogant in our opinions or that we somehow think that we've arrived.

It doesn't even mean that we think we have it all figured out (because I'm pretty sure we don't).

However, by addressing all aspects of the decision, we are now able to stand firmly on our choice to homeschool and are not shaken by negative opinions or thoughts from others.

Which brings me to our first exercise. (I know… and school hasn't even started yet, right?)

DEFINING YOUR "WHY" EXERCISE

I promise that this exercise will bring you invaluable clarity, focus (and yes, confidence) in approaching the school year.

In other words, yes, it's worth your time. And it only takes a few minutes (promise).

Check out the "Developing Your Why Journaling Prompts" in the "Activities & Printables" section in the back of this book. Here's where you'll discover several pages of questions to help you figure out your "why" and to help you make peace with the "why-nots."

Be honest about any concerns you may have about homeschooling, and come up with your own statements.

Consider this to be a brainstorming exercise. You may want to re-write your thoughts or gather them differently into a final, "more official" "why" statement. It is also helpful to have a 30-second version (an "elevator pitch" of sorts) of your homeschooling "why."

Because people will ask. Even on the elevator.

So, right now, I would encourage you to stop reading and walk through these questions.

Don't worry, I'll wait for you.

Points to Ponder

• Is this your first year as a homeschooler, or is it your fourteenth? Or perhaps somewhere in-between? If you aren't a brand-new homeschooler, how have you seen your homeschooling "why" change over the years?

• What unique aspects (either for the entire family, or for individual children) do you foresee for this coming year? How may these things change your focus or your "why" this year?

For Additional Info

• Back to School: The Most Important Thing I Want to Tell You

• Standing at the Crossroads of New Homeschool and Parenting Phase

• I Am That Mom Dealing with Homeschool Burnout

• The Great Homeschool Debate: Is Homeschooling Always Best?

Helpful Resources

• "bloom: A Journey to Joy (and Sanity) for Homeschool Moms" Online Video Course

Related Activities and Printables in This Book

• Back to School Checklist
• Developing Your Why Journaling Prompts

PART 2: CLEAN OUT AND SET UP

CHAPTER 3: CONQUERING THE CHAOS AND CLUTTER

Alright. Ready to move into the nitty-gritty of back to school prep? Yes, this is where the heavy lifting comes in. Pun totally intended. It's time to use words and phrases like cleaning out, organizing and purging. Words that aren't necessarily fun to do, but that bring great rewards when they are done.

And that's where I want you to focus your gaze right now: At an organized and neat homeschool area that is full of stuff that you actually want (and not clogged with items that you don't).

Don't think about all the details (yet). Just envision your space: A clean and beautiful place where learning can easily happen.

It doesn't have to be magazine or Pinterest-worthy. It just needs to work for you, and not against you.

THE BIG PICTURE

From last February to June, that's exactly how I felt about my homeschool area. I felt like it was working against us.

You see, due to some unforeseen and substantial circumstances around Thanksgiving last year, our homeschool was thrown into a complete tailspin as our kids switched curriculum and began attending two on-campus class days through our local charter school.

It was crazy dramatic, and it all happened within a matter of a few weeks. And it took place during the prep for the Christmas and New Year holidays.

So, in the chaos of all the events, it was all that I could do to get the kids enrolled, figure out the books and chart a new course for the second half of the year.

As a result, **our homeschool area felt like a hodgepodge** of what we'd been doing before and what we were working on now. Papers began piling up and books (some we were using and some that no longer had any purpose) were everywhere.

I knew I needed to bring order to all the madness, but **I was never quite able to catch my breath long enough to make it happen.** Running a blog, tutoring at our local co-op, launching a new e-course and homeschooling our four kiddos kept me extremely occupied (go figure).

School ended in June, and then the summer trips and various camps began. Again, no time to get in there and bring some order.

But finally… late July arrived. And that's when I finally walked into that space and said, "Oh yeah. Piles of papers? Half-completed workbooks? Unused teacher guides? Your day has come."

So in this chapter, I'm going to share with you the things I said to myself during that clean out.

We will identify the main types of clutter and chaos in a homeschool space; and one by one, I'll show you my tips to bring refreshment and order.

THE PRINTED HOMESCHOOL CURRICULUM OVERFLOW

First, I discovered that I'd become quite a collector… of the wrong kind of things.

As I mentioned previously, we had loads of half-finished curriculum. We had other resources that we'd tried and didn't work. We had re-usable learning materials that had been re-used one too many times. And then, we had more stuff that I'd bought that we'd never even gotten to.

Please tell me I'm not the only one like this. Ahem.

So. Anyway. Yes, there were lots of things that just needed to go.

And… (this was so hard for me!) *I just let them go.*

I'd like to tell you that I sold them all for hundreds of dollars on eBay or other homeschool curriculum exchange sites, but to be frank, I've only had limited success in re-selling these items online.

There were a few things that I knew would be in high demand and so I listed them. But honestly, much of it I tossed in our recycle bin. Here were a few things I kept in mind as I purged:

1. I used a paper shredder to destroy any papers that contained the kids names or any personal information.

If the information was just in one area, I ripped off that part of the paper and just shredded that. If the information was all over the page, the entire page was turned into confetti.

Random mom question: Are your kids in awe of the "magical" paper shredder? My seven and four-year-old have this weird fascination with it, so I had no shortage of volunteers to help me shred. My older boys (aged 10 and 12) lost their paper-shredder-fascination about a year ago and it is no longer a source of entertainment to them. I figure I've got a few more years left before the paper-shredder-mojo wears off with the younger ones too, so I'm making the most of it.

2. I created a file of scratch paper out of those papers without any personal info.

We go through loads of paper in our house, and often it's no big deal if there are math exercises or past school year schedules or something like that on the back. In fact, my kids usually get a kick out of whatever's on the back of their paper.

The difference this year, however, is that instead of just being a pile of papers inside a schoolroom cabinet, I decided to elevate these second-chance papers (yes, even papers need a second chance) to a pretty file folder on my desk.

Now granted, we had more papers than what would fit in the file folder, so I put the rest in a box and stored it high up and out of the way for everyday use.

3. I created a system to keep my kids' special papers and drawings in a safe place for later.

I have to tell you: These special papers (you know the ones) were one of the biggest reasons why I felt paralyzed for the longest time by the schoolroom mess. I had a huge pile of them building up and I had no clue how to organize what was there, and no plan of how to regularly handle the influx of new papers.

But I'm excited to report that I did find hope! More on that in a minute when I talk about my reckoning with "the stack."

THE DIGITAL HOMESCHOOL CURRICULUM SCAVENGER HUNT

This was both an embarrassing (and enlightening!) area to clean out.

I found oodles of goodies in my computer! Lots of things that were kind of virtually "shoved" in one folder or the other without a ton of organization.

How had these resources been right under my nose and I'd never used them?

And that's when I started feeling overwhelmed, simply because I saw all of the different options available and wasn't even sure where to start.

My heart told me the cold hard truth: **I needed to put all those good electronic resources to work (or I simply needed to delete them).**

So, in a nutshell, that's what I did.

1. I did my best to gather up all the resources and arrange them into like groups so that I could see everything in one place.

It made sense to my brain to group them by subject instead of grade or school year, but, when you do your clean out, organize them in a way that makes sense to you.

2. I took the plunge and decided to purge what we wouldn't use.

I did use some restraint, however, and kept things if I felt it might be useful to one of my kids in the next year or two. But for those resources that we'd outgrown (or that were low-quality)? Those hit the digital trash can.

3. For those items that did make the cut, I created a digital version of the "Taking Inventory of School Supplies Charts" document (learn more about

this in the "Activities and Printables" section).

By creating this digital version, I had a log of what actually was on my hard drive so that I could remember to use the resources.

4. I either printed out (or gave my kids digital access) to those e-documents that we're using this year.

Whenever possible, I tried to give the kids access to the files on their devices so that we could save a few hundred trees.

This also seemed to win mom points because, to my children, a school resource that's suddenly accessible on their Kindle or iPod is elevated to an exciting new status. Just saying.

LOTS AND LOTS OF LEARNING MATERIALS

In order to spice up our learning, I like to include lots of extra learning materials in our school activities.

This really does break up the monotony of a workbook or of just dryly reading a text. I think this approach is especially helpful in subjects like math where it's super easy to get bored with the same thing every day.

Therefore, our school room has lots of puzzles, games, hands on manipulatives and the sort.

In a later chapter, we will talk in more detail about how to organize these types of learning materials so that you can include them into a regular homeschool rhythm.

But I wanted to mention learning materials here because, if they are already in your classroom, **they may need a good clean out too.**

Here's how I physically organize these resources.

I first **sort them by subject type** (General, Language Art, History, Math, Preschool, etc); and

I dedicate a shelf (or a box, or a cabinet) to each type of learning material.

This is also a great time to take inventory on these items so that you don't have to look through them again when you go to make plans to regularly include them in your teaching.

Here's how I create and organize my learning materials inventory.

I create a spreadsheet for each subject and list all of the applicable learning materials in the left hand column.

Then I list the name of each child across the top in a separate column. If the item could potentially be used with the child this year, then I either mark an "X" or, if I'm feeling particularly ambitious, I write in how I may use the resource with the child in the upcoming school year.

3) **I print off this resource and keep it in a binder** for those days when the kids (and I) need a new way to learn something.

SCHOOL SUPPLIES GONE WILD

Chances are you've probably seen at least one (if not all three) of Disney's *Toy Story* movies. *Toy Story*'s premise (and, I'm convinced, irresistible charm) is that we get a behind-the-scenes glimpse into the everyday saga of the little plastic creatures that live in our children's rooms (and let's face it—often all over our house).

In these movies, the toys come to life when no one is watching them. Which, in real life, kind of makes sense. Because how else do we explain that a doll "magically" made its way down into the family room and decided to bring a whole platoon of army men and LEGO figures with it?

Well, after examining my school area's desk drawers, **I'm convinced that everyday school supplies like paper clips, pencils and staple removers lead an exciting secret double-life too.**

I have no idea how so many half-used crayons, rubber bands, push pins, broken ear buds, and cheap plastic pencil sharpeners made their way into my desk drawers! Truly.

I watched them multiply as our last school year progressed, but when I finally opened up my drawers again in July for the Great Clean Out, it was shocking. And mind-boggling.

I'm telling you: Disney has a multimillion dollar movie franchise just waiting to be discovered.

Anywho, there wasn't any great magic in how I cleaned up the mess.

I just simply threw away the stuff that was broken or we'd never use; and then I reorganized it again in the plastic drawer trays in a way that made sense. The kids were a great help in this.

One tip I want to share? **Open what we call the "Pencil Hospital."**

The Pencil Hospital has been a part of our schoolroom for a while now, and, in our drawer-cleaning efforts, we cleaned up (and reopened) the doors to this magical place.

I know you're asking, "What in the world is the 'Pencil Hospital'?!"

The Pencil Hospital is simply **a special box in our drawer where "sick" (dull and unsharpened) pencils reside.** Broken pencils don't come here, unless they still have enough "life" in them to be resurrected by the Pencil Hospital doctors (my kids).

Oh yes—my kids are the doctors. This means that, when someone chooses to have less than stellar behavior in our home, I sometimes choose to send them to the Pencil Hospital to "fix" (sharpen) all those pencils.

Once the pencils are fully "healthy" and restored to their proper (sharp) status, the "doctors" transfer the pencils to the regular pencil holder on my desk.

I figure it's a win-win: **We have a constant supply sharp pencils (that I don't have to sharpen) and the threat of serving in the Pencil Hospital encourages good classroom behavior.**

THE SAGA OF "THE STACK"

In every school area, there are sections where stuff just piles up.

Piles of random school schedules and field trips flyers aren't really what I'm talking about here. Those can be easily sorted through and tossed (or re-used as scratch paper).

Instead, I'm talking about **those stacks of "keepsake" papers**—drawings, reports and other items that you want to save, but have no idea of how to order or to organize.

Let me tell you my story about "the stack," and (I'm not so sorry to say) its timely demise.

For months a mounting pile of papers (which I'd dubbed "the stack") had not only taken over part of my schoolroom desk, but it had spread across the floor.

It mocked me, the stack.

It reminded me of all the cute adorable papers sitting there (papers from my kids that *I* placed there).

It told me that those papers are priceless (and that I *should* be doing something with them).

And it laughed at me because it knew that I had no idea what to do with them all.

When late July came and I was going through our classroom's great clean out, I took a long look at "the stack" and realized that, really, all I needed was a few hours and one great plan to not only eliminate "the stack" but to kick him out of our homeschool for good. And thus "My Memory Box: Kids School Paper Organizing System" was born!

I designed the kit to include four sets of the following: one 8.5 x 11-inch "My Memory Box" Box Label; fifteen 3.5 x 5-inch (approx.) Folder Labels, one for each age/grade from toddler to twelfth grade; and fifteen 2.25 x .5-inch File Folder Tabs, one for each age/grade from toddler to twelfth grade.

Each of these items are in four different colors: orange, pink, blue and green so boxes can be personalized for each child.

Along with these printables, the My Memory Box system requires the following items: a plastic file folder box; 15 hanging file folders and plastic tabs; a glue stick; and scissors and/or a paper trimmer.

To set up the system, cut everything out, glue the folder labels on the folders, glue the box label on the box; insert the file folder tabs into the plastic covers and place the folders in the box.

That's it! The My Memory Box is an easy way to treasure a child's favorite school memories, art projects, certificates, awards and other keepsakes from their toddler through teen years!

Here's a picture so you can see what it looks like.

A SANE APPROACH TO CLEANING OUT AND CLEANING UP

Can I make a few final suggestions before you start off on your organizing?

1. Be ruthless. This is especially important if space is an issue. Is it worth it to keep a bag full of science supplies if you won't use any of them this year (especially if it takes up a whole cabinet)?

2. Be practical. At the same time, be willing to consider items from your stash as substitutes for planned (but not yet purchased) school curriculum. But only keep them if you will honestly use them and give them a try. Remember, you can always try it out and get another item later if this one doesn't work!

3. Be The Tortoise. You know who The Tortoise is, right? Mr. "slow and steady wins the race" from Aesop's famous *The Tortoise and the Hare*?

So, in a nutshell: Pace yourself, and do a little at a time.

Don't try to do all of this in one day. You will walk into your homeschool space, take one look at all that's before you, and just start crying (been there, done that).

Instead, **set a goal** for when you'd like your entire area to be organized and ready to start school (use the "Back to School Checklist Planner" in the "Activities and Printables" section in the back of the book to help you plan). Then work backwards from that date.

4. Be realistic (and grace-filled) as you plan. After all, it will probably be summer when you'll be doing this, and you will have other fun and exciting things to do with your family.

I promise that this job is much less overwhelming when you just work on one aspect at a time. Set a timer, or determine to do certain areas on certain days. Make a plan that works for you and make it do-able.

Points to Ponder

• Cleaning up and clearing out your classroom is a great time to really think through what has (and has not) been working, in terms of how your supplies are set up. What do you like about the space? What can you change to make learning flow more smoothly? Do you need to add or to remove furniture (desks, a large table, more bookshelves)? In the next chapter we will discuss ideas on how to set up your school room, and so, you may find it helpful to consider these issues before then.

For Additional Info

• End of the Year Homeschool Organization: 4 Steps to Combat the Clutter

• Standing at the Crossroads of New Homeschool and Parenting Phase

• My Memory Box: New System to Organize Kids School Papers

Helpful Resources

• My Memory Box: Kids School Paper Organizer

Related Activities and Printables in This Book

• Back to School Checklist

• Taking Inventory of School Supplies Charts

CHAPTER 4: WHAT DO YOU HAVE AND WHAT DO YOU NEED?

A h, back to school. **There seems to be a near feeding frenzy that occurs this time of year for homeschoolers.** Everyone is telling us: *You need to get this curriculum! To read this book! To pick up more school supplies!* And we think: *Ah!! Oh my goodness, yes I do! Get out of my way! I need to get to the nearest Wal-Mart!*

This year, as you feel the back to school frenzy beginning to envelop you, I encourage you to stop, take a breath, and ask yourself: **What does our homeschool *really* need this year?**

And here's the great thing: If you completed a good "clean out" as prescribed in Chapter 3, you will, in fact, have a pretty good idea of what your school *does* need.

YOUR SCHOOL'S SCHEDULE

First things first: **Have you created a school calendar?**

This will of course depend on whether or not you are working with a charter school or you are filing as an independent school. Laws and regulations on these vary from state to state (and country to country), and that information is beyond the scope of this book.

You also need to **decide what type of school schedule** you will have. Will you follow the traditional school year schedule (September to June); follow a five-week-on, one-week-off-sort of schedule; or will you simple school year round? Again, this too depends on the number of school days legally required by your state or country.

Regardless, at the minimum, I'd suggest you create some sort of calendar with starting and ending school dates (if applicable), along with holidays and any breaks.

TAKING INVENTORY

Next, let's make a general plan of two things: **your child(ren)'s individual needs** (books, curriculum, other learning tools), and **your school's overall needs** (pencils, art supplies, glue sticks, etc).

And guess what? You have a great printable for that in the "Activities and Printables" section of this book! It's called the "Taking Inventory of School Supplies Charts."

There are three types of charts in this school supplies inventory: individual child charts; entire homeschool charts; and charts for co-op or other extra teaching needs.

Because we each school differently (and some subjects may require a range of books and supplies), I've created a few different templates that will work when determining each child's needs (and how your current supplies might meet those needs).

Each document contains a column where you can make a plan on how to get that particular supply (if it is needed). Customize these charts to work for you!

TIPS FOR A SUCCESSFUL SET UP

Please hear me loud and clear: **Your homeschool area does not have to look like anything formal.**

It's not even essential that you have a specific homeschool area!

In fact, even though my family does have a homeschool area, there are many days that we don't go there and do school. We find that **school can happen anywhere—inside or outside of our home.**

However, some structure and order is a good thing, especially when it comes to all the "stuff" we collect as part of our home educating.

Therefore, even if you don't have a formal homeschool area, I would highly suggest you **create some sort of general landing place** for books and supplies.

Here are some general guidelines for physically establishing a homeschool area.

1. Give each child a box for their books, folders and other supplies.

This one organizing tip will save you tons of heartache. Yes, your kids will sometimes leave their books in other places, but if you've established a general location for all workbooks, notebooks, folders and reading materials, then you can at least establish some sense of order for their individual supplies.

I prefer to use those large fabric storage bins you see at home organizing stores or online here. I would suggest you purchase boxes that measure at least 12 x 12 inches and that are fairly sturdy. Each child should have his own box.

2. Create an organized school supply area.

Where should your kids go if they need a pencil? A stapler? Glue sticks? Scissors? We have specific locations in our school area where my kids know they can go to locate these supplies.

I also would encourage you to establish one central location for all art supplies (construction paper, drawing paper, crayons, paints, paint brushes, etc). Not only will it save your sanity when it comes to doing special hands-on projects, but your kids will be able to help themselves to the supplies when creative inspiration strikes. That is, of course, if you're OK with them having free access to these supplies.

3. Create more than one suggested place to learn.

Our kids have **a few areas where they can do school**: A large kitchen-style table in our homeschool area; a couch in our homeschool area; and individual desks in their rooms. I like to give them a few formal options for doing school, and each location serves a different purpose.

We have general times in our school day (and thus general locations) for both independent and group work.

For **independent teaching times** (whether that's me working with them one-on-one, or them working through the material by themselves), we give them a few options: working at the kitchen-style table (perhaps with noise-cancelling headphones if necessary); working at their individual in-room desks or in their beds; or, if they desire additional privacy, working in another quiet place in the house such as the family room couch.

I have a formal sitting area in my master bedroom where I like to do one-on-one teaching with the kids. And sometimes, if it's a really beautiful day outside, we sit on our patio and do schoolwork. It's also a common occurrence in our home for a child to be working at our real kitchen table while I'm getting dinner started or feeding another child. Really, there's no right or wrong place to let the learning happen!

We've found it helpful for us to have our **group teaching times** at the kitchen-style table in the school area or on the couch in the homeschool area. There are several whiteboards and a map in front of the kitchen table (which come in handy for group teaching); and the couch is a great place for snuggling together to read a book.

We often find ourselves on the couch too if I'm reading from a science text (for example) and the older boys are taking notes. I can easily read and write suggested notes on a hand-held whiteboard. The kids sit next to me and copy what I'm writing.

And during our morning Bible time, we usually all stretch out on the large family room sofa.

Do you get my point? I'm saying that it's incredibly helpful to have several types of established learning locations in your home. This is especially true if you have a large number of children you're schooling.

4. Build a home library.

Collecting books isn't usually something that we homeschoolers have to think about. It's kind of one of those inherent aspects of teaching.

However, I would challenge you to **create a central location for your reading materials** so that kids can easily see what's there. We have several shelves of both fiction and non-fiction reading for our kids to peruse during their daily reading time. Non-fiction books are arranged by subject, while fiction books are arranged by collection (author or series) or by general age group.

A well-organized home library is also an excellent way to supplement your regular teaching materials. For example, we are going to study the Middle Ages and the Renaissance this year, and I was pleased to discover that I had several books and guidebooks I'd collected on this time period when I traveled to England a few years ago.

5. Set up a library box.

I could not run my homeschool without our local library. Truly.

I'm guessing you feel the same way?

But, oh! The chaos and clutter that can ensue with library books! Especially when there are four little sets of hands digging through the pile and everyone is accessing the books at different times for different reasons.

From the beginning, **our homeschool has had a library box and that one tool has been a lifesaver for keeping all the books in one spot.**

It's nothing fancy—just a large wicker box something like this. However, it's the landing place for our library reading materials.

It's also an excellent way to transport books back and forth to the library. In fact, I pretty much feel naked walking into the library without it!

6. Make extra learning activities easily available as well.

Obviously, one of the challenges of homeschooling more than one child is that you can't be in more than one place at once.

Which means that you have to not only encourage independent learning (which I'd argue is an essential skill anyway), you have to create some sort of rhythm for the learning times where you can trade off in teaching students one-on-one and in teaching them as a group.

We're going to spend a few chapters in this book talking about how to set up a school day with a mindset I call "rhythm-based homeschooling", so I'm not going to discuss this topic in depth right now.

However, I mention it here because, in this give-and-take of independent and group teaching, there occasionally will be times when a child needs your help with an assignment and you aren't able to offer it immediately because you're helping another child.

When my kids are in this situation, I've asked them to either move on to another aspect of that day's assignment or to work on assignments from another subject.

But there are times when they are finished with all their other assignments for the day and require hands-on help for other subjects that day. In this situation, I'm not ready to release them to other non-school activities yet because I find that it can be really hard to reel them back in later.

So, we've brainstormed some general learning activity ideas that they can do in the meantime while they are waiting. These usually consist of games, activities or other out-of-the-box things they can do to reinforce other learning concepts.

You'll find a list of our favorite learning games and learning tools here.

I try to keep these activities together in one place so that the kids can quickly find something to occupy themselves for a few minutes.

I actually got this idea from a friend of mine who used to be an elementary school teacher. She would set up various "learning stations" around her classroom (large puzzles to complete, for example) and she told her students that if they finished an assignment before the allotted time had ended, then they could quietly work on an activity of their choice at one of the learning stations.

I had to adopt that one in my home classroom!

MAKE A SHOPPING LIST

You've purged all that you don't need.

You've set up foundational areas of your homeschool area to encourage learning and keep things organized.

Now it's time for the fun part: shopping!

By completing the "Taking Inventory of School Supplies" Chart you will be able to identify what exactly you need to buy—including curriculum for each child, school supplies for your classroom, and school supplies for any co-ops or group teaching.

If you need some curriculum inspiration, check out this ultimate list of homeschool resources, along with another list here of some of our favorite homeschooling curriculum by subject.

In terms of purchasing basic school supply needs, I am a huge advocate of buying school supplies at the dollar store!

I know there are seasonal back to school supplies sales at the big box stores, but honestly? I prefer to get it all at once at the dollar store, and I'll tell you why:

- Everything is in one place at the dollar store (no need to run to multiple stores)

- No need to wait for a sale at the dollar store (yep, it's all always a dollar!)

- You don't have to deal with the crazy rush at those other stores during those back to school sales (last year there was a line to go down the back to school aisles at my local Wal-Mart. No joke.)

- No need to "hope" that those other stores have what you're looking for (last year I couldn't even find what I was looking for because there were literally just piles and piles of stuff all over the back to school supplies section).

I figure that if I pay an extra 50 cents for my crayons this year because I go to the dollar store (instead of waiting for the annual back to school supplies sales) then it is totally worth it!! That 50 cents is worth my sanity, my time and my gasoline!

To make your shopping a breeze (and to make sure you have all the supplies you can think of) I have compiled a very, very helpful resource: The Dollar Store School Supply Shopping List !

This invaluable, seven-page, full-color printable contains a four-page shopping list that categorizes all of your necessary back-to-school items—all found at the Dollar Store. There are 191 items are grouped into 14 categories for shopping ease.

This is one of those sanity-savers that make the back-to-school-shopping experience so much easier! You'll want to grab this one.

MY 13 MUST-HAVE HOMESCHOOL ITEMS

Don't you love it when people share their "hacks"—ways to use everyday items to solve everyday dilemmas?

I've discovered a few invaluable school supplies that have truly revolutionized how I teach, and I'd like to share them with you here.

You may be already using (or plan to use) some of these supplies. But a few of these may be those you haven't thought of.

Dry erase boards. I can't emphasize enough how much I use these, both the large, wall-mounted ones and the handheld ones. I use them to write assignments, demonstrate a math problem, to aid in note taking—you name it. I also love the dry-erase writing practice boards you can get (picture these as a dry-erase form of one or two of those dotted-lines writing areas on manuscript paper).

Countdown timer. I love having timers in our teaching time because it motivates kids to finish up and to stay on track. This is our favorite countdown timer because it visually shows the time getting smaller (the red area visually decreases as the time winds down).

Noise canceling headphones. I have a few students who really need silence in order to work, and we have found noise-canceling headphones to be a lifesaver so that several kids can work in one room at once.

Diffuser with essential oils. I recently began using essential oils in our home, and wow, there are so many applications! I like to use a diffuser in our classroom so that the scent permeates the air and sets the tone for a calm, focused learning environment. Some of my favorite oils for classroom use include Lavender (to calm), Peppermint (to wake up), Lemon (to freshen and cheer), and a blend called Joy (to help keep the grouches at bay).

Online calendar planner. I have experimented with several in the past, but have found Homeschool Planet to be the easiest and most user-friendly. You can read my review of this online homeschool planner here.

Map of the U.S. (or whichever country you live in); and map of the world or globe. We reference our map of the U.S. all the time! It seems like I'm constantly using it (or our map of the world or our globe) to share more in-depth about a subject. Yes, we use it for geography, but I'm telling you—it comes up all the time in almost every subject! And I just think it's good to have a map constantly up for kids to see. It's a great way to (passively) get basic geographic concepts in their brain.

Analog clock. We have a large analog wall clock in our school area which helps keep us focused and on task. We basically use it to make us aware of the "pillars" we've set up for our day (more on "pillars" in future chapters). And I prefer using an analog clock because it helps the little ones practice telling time!

A monthly meal plan. At the beginning of each month I compile a list of meals for the next 4-5 weeks. This may sound super overwhelming, but I promise it can be super easy with an awesome meal planning website called Plan to Eat. I have used Plan to Eat for almost three years now and I can't say enough good things about it! The site allows you to store your recipes and then drag and drop them into the specific calendar dates. When it comes time to create a grocery list, you choose the dates you want to shop for and it auto-populates a list of ingredients for you into a shopping list with items categorized by store. Seriously a lifesaver!

Once a month shopping trip. Once I've created my monthly meal plan, then I take a day to go to three different stores and gather all the supplies. Yes, it makes for a long day, but it feels *amazing* to have all our supplies for the month in the house and ready to go. I don't have to think about it for another month! I do run out to the store maybe one more time to gather produce and other perishable items. We also are members of a local farm co-op where we have fresh organic veggies delivered every week. We save money by only going to those stores once a month or so too because there's less opportunity to buy all those extra items at the store.

Crockpot. This little time-saving kitchen appliance makes homemade dinner possible for me on the most hectic of school days. It has saved me *many* times from a trip through a drive-thru. In fact, I purposely plan crock pot meals on those days when I know we'll be running from sun-up to sun-down doing homeschool activities and sports practices. My all-time favorite crock pot is the Hamilton Beach Stovetop Slow Cooker because the insert can be used on the stove! This means that I can *use only one pot* to caramelize onions and brown meat on the stove before I put it in the slow cooker. It also means that I can cook up something quickly if I get it into the crock pot late and I need to get dinner on the table pronto. And speaking of quick and easy meals…

Freezer meals. Oh, it's lovely to have a stash of meals ready to go at a moment's notice! I try to include at least three or four recipes in our monthly meal planning that can be freezer meals. I usually make two to three batches of each freezer meal recipe on a family meal prep day (when we work as a family to create freezer meals). My favorite freezer meal book is Fix, Freeze, Feast: The Delicious, Money-Saving Way to Feed Your Family.

Simple systems for household tasks. I love developing systems that allow us to streamline regular tasks. For our family, some of those include a once-a-day pick-up (where we clean up our main living area and our school room); and a regular laundry day (usually Sunday). These two things alone help keep our home picked up (and save my sanity).

A regular time of prayer and meditation in the Bible. There's one final thing that is perhaps the most essential part of our homeschool day, and that's our time together in the Bible. I do my best to spend time with God first thing in the morning (sometimes using a devotional like Jesus Calling: Enjoying Peace in His Presence to guide my time), and then we spend time learning together as a family. This centers and grounds us and reminds us of our greater purposes in this life. It changes up from season to season, but currently we use Jesus Calling: 365 Devotions for Kids; and Bible Road Trip to teach our kids.

Points to Ponder

• Dream for a moment: What would your ideal homeschool area look like? What would it contain and how would it be set up? Now think about reality. How can you incorporate some of those dreams into your current homeschool environment?

• What are your must-have homeschool items? What would you add to the list?

For Additional Info

• What A Crock! 5 New Uses for This Mighty Appliance

• Homeschool Sanity Savers Part 1: Monthly Meal Planning, Monthly Shopping and the Crock Pot

• How to Have Your Own Family Meal Prep Day

• How to Make Your Own Freezer Meals (16 Tips and 2 Recipes)

• Homeschool Sanity Savers Part 2: Daily and Weekly Household Routines That Work for Your Family

• The Ultimate Guide to Homeschool Planning: Tips and Top Resources for Scheduling Success

• Awesome Learning Tools and Learning Games

• Ultimate Homeschool Resources: Freebies, Ideas, Books, Printables and More!

• Recommended Homeschooling Resources

Helpful Resources

• Dry Erase Boards: wall-mounted, handheld, and writing practice boards

• Countdown timer

• Noise-canceling headphones

• Diffuser

• My favorite essential oils

• Homeschool Planet online homeschool planner

- Map of the US, Map of the World and Globe
- Plan to Eat meal planning membership
- Fix, Freeze, Feast: The Delicious, Money-Saving Way to Feed Your Family
- Hamilton Beach Stovetop Slow Cooker
- Analog wall clock
- Resources to help kids learn to tell time
- Jesus Calling: Enjoying Peace in His Presence
- Jesus Calling: 365 Devotions for Kids
- Bible Road Trip
- Dollar Store Back to School Supplies Shopping List

Related Activities and Printables in This Book

- Back to School Checklist
- Taking Inventory of School Supplies Charts

PART 3: BUILD RHYTHM AND LEARNING PLANS

CHAPTER 5:
RHYTHMS NOT SCHEDULES:
AN INTRO TO RHYTHM-BASED
HOMESCHOOLING

I f you hang out in the homeschooling world long enough you'll quickly realize that **many of us have specific opinions about how to structure (or not structure) a homeschool day.** I have operated on both extremes of this thinking, experimenting with both a rigid, hour-by-hour schedule and free-form, open learning times. And you know what I've discovered?

Neither one works (at least not for my family).

Let me back up and tell you my perceptions about each of these approaches.

First, the hour-by-hour schedule felt very comfortable and predictable to me. It's much easier to meet a goal when you have a detailed plan, right?

As a former magazine managing editor, schedules made sense to me. I loved that I could tell you that on Tuesday at 2:15 p.m. we'd be doing math together. **Having a schedule gave me great, great comfort and confidence** that yes, I could actually do this homeschool thing.

But, as I detailed in Plan to Be Flexible, having a tight, rigid homeschool schedule was my ultimate undoing. It set up expectations that could never have been met, and left both my kids and me feeling like a failure (daily) for not being able to meet the goals that a piece of paper had told us we needed to meet.

So I switched to the opposite extreme and decided to **just "let learning happen" for my kids with an open schedule.**

It did not take long for me to realize that this wasn't a good fit for us either. I know several families who can school like this successfully, but honestly, I felt like our homeschool had no direction or focus and that drove me insane. I had a really hard time prepping for what to teach and my kids desired more direction from me.

So…there I was: I was convinced that we needed to homeschool our kids, but I had no earthly clue of how to do it!

RHYTHM-BASED HOMESCHOOLING: A MIDDLE-OF-THE-ROAD APPROACH

I did some soul-searching and wrote down a few things that, in a perfect world, **I wanted to be able to have in our homeschooling:**

- I wanted to be organized and purposeful with our learning.

- I wanted to have some sort of realistic plan for the day that accounted for the unexpected realities of homeschool life.

- I wanted to include fun, hands-on learning projects and for my kids to have the opportunity to follow rabbit trails and enjoy unplanned learning.

- I longed to build self-motivated kids that loved learning… and yet, I found myself shutting down their requests to dig in the garden or to explore a topic online because we needed to "stick to the schedule."

I couldn't imagine life without our homeschool schedule; and yet, deep down, I knew that **most days it left me feeling like a drill sergeant that never could quite get his recruits to follow along.** Despite all my planning, rearranging (and coaxing), most days I still felt like I got never got enough done.

But what about all those wonderful things I'd pinned on my Pinterest board! These were wonderful learning activities that I knew my kids would love to do! Couldn't we somehow find time for these?

Wasn't this what homeschooling was about, for Pete's sake?!

RHYTHM-BASED HOMESCHOOLING: THE SMALL SHIFT THAT CHANGED EVERYTHING

And one day it dawned on me: **Isn't there a way to enjoy the benefits of both scheduled and un-scheduled learning?**

There has to be some sort of happy medium here, right?

So after loads of experimentation, I **developed a revolutionary approach that allowed for the best aspects of both scheduled and unscheduled homeschooling: rhythm-based homeschooling.**

Rhythm-based homeschooling isn't a method really, but instead a set of key principles that are adaptable for any family, whether they tend to be more naturally structured or unstructured in their learning. No two days are the same in homeschooling, and rhythm-based homeschooling is flexible enough to accommodate for this.

Rhythm-based homeschooling walks the line of setting homeschooling goals while offering grace for the times when those goals aren't met. It also allows for a family to have **a regular flow to the day without the baggage of a moment-by-moment account of activities.**

To best understand the ins-and-outs of rhythm-based homeschooling, I suggest you take my online video course "Rhythm: Guiding Your Family to Their Ideal Learning Flow." Along with three pre-recorded video training sessions, "rhythm" offers 38 pages of indepth exercises, resources and life-changing activities so that you can discover practical, customized solutions that you can immediately implement in your homeschool.

However, I wanted to share with you here **a few key principles here that can get you started on the road of rhythm-based homeschooling.**

FOUR FOUNDATIONAL CONCEPTS OF A HOMESCHOOL RHYTHM

There are two key concepts that work together to maintain a healthy rhythm: pillars with boundaries, and goals with grace.

As we define each of these concepts individually, you will quickly recognize how "pillars" and "boundaries" work together, and "goals" and "grace" work together. You will also see how all four of these concepts join as one to build a beautiful network of a healthy rhythm.

1. Pillars

Pillars are simply key, habitual practices that frame the contents of our days.

To explain the concept of pillars, allow me to use the example of building a home. When constructing a dwelling, we first need to have core pillars in place to support the structure.

We each have different houses (and of course different activity goes on in the different houses) but there are foundational pillars—a sense of order and structure--in each of our dwellings. The house would fall down without these key elements.

So, the first step in creating a rhythm is to create key pillars in our day. These could be things like "sleeping/waking"; "meals/eating"; and "rest time." These pillars are set at approximate times (for example, breakfast is at 8:00 a.m. and lunch is at 12:00 p.m.) and the learning flows around them.

In our school, we start school off together with our Bible time, and then learning flows from there depending on what we're studying, the deadlines we're facing and the day's other tasks (for example, do we have a doctor's appointment, a field trip and/or science experiments?). We flow like this until lunch, and then we finish up the rest of the day's activities after lunch.

If you'd like a little more structure with the teaching times, you can consider having mini pillars in the day for your teaching time, such as a time every day where you will learn a subject together (for us, that's History or Science). But, you don't have to be super strict or scheduled about this if that's not comfortable or realistic.

At the end of our morning time, the kids and I discuss how today will flow based on that day's activities. The kids all are aware of their assignments found in their Homeschool Planet tracking software, so once we've checked in to make sure they don't have any questions about their first tasks, I release them to begin working. Then I systematically begin working one-on-one with each of them as their needs require.

2. Boundaries

Boundaries are those practices we establish to keep pillars strong.

We need these mental attitudes (specific thought patterns we will begin to adapt) and tangible activities (actual tasks we will or will not do) as general supports to reinforce the pillars. This is where the idea of pillars goes from being merely theoretical to the actual.

Let's talk specifics and examine what it looks like for pillars and boundaries to work together. How can a boundary be used to reinforce the pillar of sleeping/waking times, for example? I've categorized these actions as mental attitudes or tangible activities:

Mental attitudes (boundaries that strengthen the sleeping/waking pillar):

• I remember why I wake at a specific time. For example, I remind myself that when I rise early before the children, I have a chance to focus, to calm my mind and to pray, which prepares me for the best teaching day possible.

• I remember why I ask the kids to wake at a specific time. For example, when they rise on time, it allows time for them to complete their morning chores; it helps them to establish a strong sleep/wake cycle; and it helps support the eating/meals pillar because we are ready to eat by a certain time, which in turn, helps us get our school day started by a certain time.

Tangible activities (boundaries that strengthen the sleeping/waking pillar):

• I set my alarm to wake up before the kids so that I can be prepared and take care of the activities mentioned in the "mental attitudes" boundary; and

• The children set alarms for themselves so that they can wake at a specific time and take care of their activities mentioned in the "mental attitudes" boundary.

3. Goals

Goals are those long or short term plans that we make. Goals are the guiding factors of our homeschool—the *what* we will attempt do in our days. They're the target that we shoot for.

What is the ultimate end goal of our homeschooling? What are our individual goals for each child, both now in this season and overall in the long term?

Once these goals are defined we can bring purpose and clarity about what we will and will not involve our kids in. This purpose determines how we're going to fill our days: which extra-curricular activities are a good fit; which curriculum choices will help the child accomplish his overall goals, etc.

However, goals can sometimes have a flip side: goals can be lofty, idealistic concepts that exist solely on paper (which renders them meaningless); or goals can make us feel guilty (a list of ways that we're not measuring up). Goals are incredibly powerful for helping us shape our destinies, but we have to hold them with an open hand that allows for the realities of life to happen.

4. Grace

We mentioned above the inherent flaws in goal making. It's in these flawed areas where we see the concept of "grace" shine.

Grace is the ability to forgive imperfection and to allow "real life" to happen. Grace allows us to give ourselves space and permission for the goals or plans we've made to not turn out perfectly.

Grace means that we do our best to not set ourselves up for unrealistic expectations.

However, an atmosphere of grace requires faith. If we were to use the analogy of goals being arrows that we aim at a target, grace gives us the confidence to believe that if we keep shooting those arrows as straight as we (imperfectly) can, it will all turn out well.

In a realistic homeschool environment, grace can be translated as acceptance of the imperfection: acceptance of the good days, the bad days, the days with behavior issues, the days when we're sick, and the days when we just don't think we can do it anymore.

A BEAUTIFUL HARMONY

"Pillars with boundaries" and "goals with grace" are concepts that serve as the science behind our school rhythm. They are the starting point for determining how we can guide our children's individual learning rhythms.

I've just scratched the surface here of "rhythm-based homeschooling," but I pray that you're able to see the vision for this revolutionary way of thinking about a homeschool day.

Points to Ponder

• If you have homeschooled previously, what have been your experiences with scheduled and unscheduled learning?

• Does the concept of "rhythm-based homeschooling" appeal to you? How could implementing the concepts of "pillars with boundaries" and "goals with grace" change how your homeschool operates?

For Additional Info

• 8 Ways to Encourage Child Led Learning in Your Homeschool

• Pinterest Board: Kids Projects & Kids Activities

• "…but am I doing enough homeschool?" Homeschooling Through the Tough Seasons

• No More Waking Up to Chaos: Tips for Moms to Start Each Day Off On the Right Foot

Helpful Resources

• "Rhythm: Guiding Your Family to Their Ideal Learning Flow" Online Video Course

• Homeschool Planet online homeschool planner

• Plan to Be Flexible

• Vibrant Homeschooling's Pinterest Boards

Related Activities and Printables in This Book

• Back to School Checklist

• Pillars and Boundaries Chart

• Goals with Grace Chart

CHAPTER 6: HOW TO CREATE A LIVING SUBJECT PLAN

When I first started homeschooling, I used an all-in-one curriculum that gave a highly detailed list of daily activities for every subject. I was told that this was supposed to "free" me, because now I didn't need to create my own school schedule.

It all sounded good until I actually started going through the curriculum and realized that **my family—or anyone's family, for that matter—could not perfectly accomplish the schedule the curriculum had laid out!**

Although the curriculum itself was challenging and filled with quality material, I found it extremely difficult to discern daily assignments because **our days never perfectly matched up with what the curriculum had scheduled for us.**

Was this the curriculum's fault per se? Not really.

The problem was that the curriculum's rigid schedule pigeonholed my week into an awkwardly-sized, unworkable shape. Like an oddly-sized garment that was loose in some areas and tight in others, this one- sized-all, pre-fixed schedule was clearly one- size-fits-none. I was tired of the extra time I spent tailoring this supposedly "time- saving schedule" to fit my family's natural learning flow.

What I really needed was **a detailed subject plan that was organized and purposeful, yet flexible enough** to allow for exploratory learning, last-minute project ideas and the occasional hiccup in our week.

BUILDING ONGOING LEARNING AND READING LISTS

Here was another problem I encountered: For a handful of subjects (for me that's history, science and math), **I also needed some sort of document that gathered all the potential learning materials.** Yes, this would include textbooks and "official" curriculum, but it would also include resources gathered from Pinterest and other online resources.

I create columns within the document to house each of these different learning avenues: "Supplemental Books," "Websites," "Online games/iPad Apps," "Online Videos/Movies," "Field Trips," etc.

I call this document the "Learning Resource Grid," (more on that in a few paragraphs) and you can find it in the "Activities & Printables" section in the back.

I also saw many links to great fiction books (often listed by grade) on Pinterest. Yet, for the longest time, I had no idea what to do with these book lists. I wanted to incorporate them into our curriculum, but it seemed like I had no general way to organize the titles and then make a plan for what I wanted my children to read this year.

However, I began gathering these resources into grades or subject and then creating master reference spreadsheets for each. **You can find a blank version of the "Grade-Level Reading List Charts (Fiction, Non-Fiction and Family Read-Aloud)" in the "Activities & Printables" section.**

Once this "Learning Resource Grid" and the "Grade Level Reading List Chart" were developed, I could pull ideas from these sources into what I call our weekly "Subject Plan."

Let's talk more about what a "Subject Plan" is, and how it can create a flexible homeschool learning rhythm.

BUILDING A FLEXIBLE SUBJECT PLAN

It took me several years, but eventually I transitioned into a new way of organizing my curriculum plans.

Instead of a moment-by-moment daily schedule of pre-determined curriculum content, I create a "Subject Plan": **a document that outlines the general topics for each subject, and lists potential activities for those topics.**

What is the difference between a "Subject Plan" and the other charts mentioned in the previous section?

The "Subject Plan" is the general action plan that you will take for the week. It lists the activities that you (probably) will do and is determined only 2-4 weeks in advance.

Think of it this way: The "Learning Resource Grid" and the "Grade-Level Reading List Charts" are the locations to store lots of ideas, while the "Subject Plan" is the potential implementation plan of some of those ideas.

There's still room for options in the Subject Plan, and that's because I prefer to give room for our days to naturally determine the actual assignments. Keeping the Subject Plan loose allows for personal choice (I can direct our children to assignments that I know they'll enjoy); freedom (I can choose whether or not an assignment will be a good fit for our week); and flexibility (I can incorporate new ideas or resources anytime into our plan).

However, the Subject Plan is still a necessary step because it narrows down all the choices into a manageable list of learning activities for a specific time period.

Let's look more closely as to how these charts can work together to create a flexible learning rhythm. We'll use Science as an example.

1. Develop a Subject Learning Ideas List.

Let's say that we're going to study Anatomy this year. Therefore, first, I come up with a rough list of the content to cover such as "the Brain and Nervous System," "the Heart and Circulatory System," "the Lungs and Respiratory System" and so on. Preferably, this topical list would at least partially come from a main science textbook on Anatomy. I consider this main textbook my "spine" or "core curriculum" for the subject.

2. Connect topics to approximate dates in the Subject Learning Ideas list.

Next, using the dates from our school calendar, I add in the approximate dates that we'll be studying each topic. For example, "The Brain and Nervous System" topic might become September 1-12 (week one and two of our school year), while "the Heart and

Circulatory System" topic could be assigned to September 15-26 (weeks three and four).

3. Connect activities and resources to topics and dates.

Then, I begin plugging ideas into the Subject Learning Ideas list. This is where the treasure hunt begins! While a strong curriculum core provides much of the content ideas, I enjoy digging around to find other unique ways to learn a topic.

So, for example, if I find a great online video of how the heart beats, I would paste the link in the column "Online Videos/Movies" in the row that contains the topic "The Heart and Circulatory System." The name of a pop-up book about the division of the brain would be listed under the column "Supplemental Books," in the row "The Brain and Nervous System," and so on. You could include as many additional details here as you like, for example: "pages 14-18," "library book to borrow," "Netflix movie," or "buy this book on Amazon."

A GROWING AND CHANGING SUBJECT PLAN

The key here is not to reach a point where you state, "I have gathered absolutely every resource and curriculum idea for this subject." Instead, I prefer to have specific "gathering" periods throughout the year when I gather ideas in the Subject Plan document.

1. Back to School.

In the summer, as part of my back to school planning, I gather the core school books and determine the main topics we want to cover. If there's a supplemental resource that I know we will use for multiple weeks, I consider purchasing it as well. At this time, I also try to plug in as many ideas as possible into the subject plan, especially for the topics covered in the first month or two of school. Like a parent pushing a child on his first two-wheeled bike ride, these activities give me a good push toward what will happen this year.

2. Two to three weeks before a new topic.

A few weeks before we start a new topic, I intensify my "activity gathering" process again. This is when I look online again for resources, review the specific books available at my library and gather ideas.

3. The Sunday before.

Right before the week begins, I review what topic we'd planned to cover and the ideas I've gathered. I make an extremely loose structure of how the activities might work out, based on what may be going on that week.

For example, for History, I may determine that on Monday, we'll read from our core book about Western Expansionism in the 1850s and talk about questions on page 118; on Wednesday we'll make a map that details the Oregon Trail and play an online game; and on Thursday, we'll build a covered wagon from an idea I've got on my Pinterest boards.

FLEXIBILITY, FREEDOM (AND TRUE LEARNING)

The week may work out exactly like this...or it may not! This is a general outline and if something isn't working, you can always switch in another activity from your Subject Plan that might work better.

Most importantly, don't make it your goal to complete every project idea! Completing everything on your Subject Plan is not a true measure of successfully teaching a topic. Instead, ask yourself, "Did the child connect with the material in a meaningful way? Did they gain knowledge and express it in ways that will help them retain that information?" These are the true marks of successfully learning a given topic.

You can create these types of spreadsheets for each subject you cover. Or...not. Some subjects are super easy to plan and may just consist of working through a single book or curriculum without any additional outside resources.

Pick and choose the subjects where you really want to have multiple learning options. Don't make yourself crazy and do this for every single subject, especially with multiple kids!

Overall, having a Subject Plan provides structured and purposeful learning (important in helping us reach those annual or big-picture goals we've outlined) without the constraints of a predetermined, moment-by- moment plan. It is a living, flexible way to effectively organize and plan curriculum.

Points to Ponder

• Which subjects do you feel would best be supported by a "Subject Plan"? How could having options in your homeschool day and week bring more peace, joy and creativity to your learning environment?

For Additional Info

• Rhythm-Based Homeschooling: A Practical, Customized Approach

• 17 Awesome Pinterest Boards for Homeschooling Encouragement, Ideas, Activities and Crafts

Helpful Resources

• Vibrant Homeschooling's Pinterest Boards

Related Activities and Printables in This Book

• Learning Resource Grid

• Grade-Level Reading List Charts (Fiction, Non-Fiction and Family Read-Aloud)

• Subject Plan

CHAPTER 7: BASIC TIPS FOR DAILY SUCCESS

As summer ends and fall approaches, the feeling of fresh starts and new opportunities is nearly intoxicating. And as we begin our back to school preparations, we realize that time away from the books (or at least away from the routine) has hopefully brought some refreshment and new vision. We're eager to listen to new ideas (and to share the good ones we've discovered).

And of course all the new "stuff"—curriculum, workbooks, even normally drab items like dry-erase boards—just add to the festive atmosphere.

We find room to dream, to hope and to envision what our school *could* be like. We say things like: *This year I'm going to go on more field trips! Make more time for crafts! Do more experiments! You know—our family is really going to* experience *learning!*

Or maybe we make promises to ourselves like: *I'm going to be more cheerful! Be more organized! Have my lessons prepped and ready weeks in advance!*

Things are going to be different, we say. And we mean it.

The plans are big and the goals are great. And that's super!

But what I see happening year after year (and I fall right into this category too) is **a really ugly, disappointing fall-from-grace come late September/early October.**

About a month into the school year we notice a few things: the shininess of the new books has rubbed off; the curriculum may not be running as smoothly as we'd thought; **and we realize, hey—someone gave us the same kids as last year (with all of their same idiosyncrasies)!**

And so we sit, mid-to-late-September, with a lapful of fallen hopes and heavy frustration. Our soul is saddened and crushed as we watch our idyllic homeschool planning crash head-on with our very imperfect and messy realities.

And that, my friends, is why many of us find ourselves entrenched in the same habits and schooling atmospheres year after year.

We may dream of a different way of doing things (which is great) and make attempts to change, but so often come early October we find ourselves back where we were last year.

Who wants to dream, we wonder, when all it leads is to heartbreak, and it seems like nothing ever changes?

I've so been there. And it's not a pretty place.

10 HELPFUL MINDSETS FOR BACK TO SCHOOL PLANNING

First of all, I don't want to give pat, easy answers because that would just be downright wrong. Often there aren't easy solutions to these ongoing homeschooling issues, so I'm not going to try to come up with some.

But can I share some mindsets that might be helpful? I feel comfortable in suggesting these here (without risking sounding flippant) because let me tell you—I'm saying them to myself as much as I am sharing them with you.

1. Choose specific, achievable goals for your homeschool planning.

Instead of making blanket statements like "We're going to do more experiments and crafts this year," create quantifiable (and achievable) milestones. For example, a better perspective might be to say "let's plan to do one science experiment with each new lesson" or "When we get home from basketball practice on Thursday afternoons, let's have a craft time where we each work on an ongoing craft project." This way, the goals aren't quite so nebulous and difficult to meet.

2. Consider the season.

Often I find that I set myself up for disaster when I simply ignore my reality!

I learned this lesson two years ago when we decided to sell our home and buy a new one. It took an immense amount of mental and physical energy to endure the buying/ selling process! As a result, I was forced to lighten our school load some weeks during that season.

I realized that something had to give, and in order to keep my sanity, my school visions and plans had to be downshifted slightly.

And you know what? We came through it just fine (and the kids caught right back up with their studies after the move).

3. Give yourself grace.

Even in the most ideal situations (without any outside drama), school can be challenging. If things don't work out just as you'd expected, take a deep breath, dust off your knees and keep on trying. Have a "Plan B" in place, and don't be afraid to use it.

Also, instead of looking at the circumstance as a "pass/fail," celebrate the good progress that has been made toward the goal (even if it's small).

4. Let your kids know what's expected of them.

I've found that my kids are more successful at completing their learning assignments when they have a checklist and a way to organize their tasks. Homeschool Planet (an online homeschool planner) is an excellent way to not only schedule out and track assignments, but to keep kids accountable (they can access their assignment portal via a laptop or handheld device).

5. Track progress and celebrate success.

Homeschooling is hard work—for you *and* for your kids!

I try to encourage my children whenever possible in their learning by rewarding them with special gifts, a trip out for ice cream, or even something as simple as recognition with the "You Are Special Today" Red Plate at dinner (the Red Plate is a special plate meant to honor accomplishments).

Success doesn't have to be determined by meeting a huge goal. I think it's incredibly important to celebrate everyday miracles and small victories with our kids.

6. Welcome (and ask for) your children's input.

What do your kids want to learn about? What's fascinating to them? As much as possible, try to develop learning opportunities that pique their curiosity. We host end-of-the-year dates with our kids to gather this information; and we also do our best to watch their cues/signals to determine how well the current learning style/topics are working.

I do want to add, however, that first, sometimes there are subjects and topics that kids need to learn that might not be their favorite (and that's alright); and second, remember that you are the teacher and have the authority to make the final call on what is taught (and how it's taught) in your school.

7. Take breaks if you need it.

This was something I fought when I first started as a homeschooler (my book Plan to Be Flexible talks about this).

I had this crazy expectation that if I planned it, it would happen.

I'd forgotten the human factor: kids get tired or squirmy; mamas get grouchy; people get sick; learning doesn't always come easy; sibling squabbles happen and character issues need to be address; and, in general, life happens.

There are many, many times when you just have to push pause on homeschooling, and that's OK. It helped me to remember that **our homeschooling was a lifestyle that worked into our family's flow and not a tyrant that demanded to be served.**

Yes, keep on track for your learning goals for the year, but be realistic. And with that in mind…

8. Remember that relationships and character building trump book learning.

My friend, a mom of eight and homeschooler for over twenty years, shared with me a long time ago that homeschooling is like a cupcake.

She explained that when you first start out you think that the book learning is the "cake" part of the cupcake (and thus is the essential part of homeschooling), while the relationships gained with your children is the "frosting" (the extra part at the end that is an added benefit).

However, she says that, in fact, relationships are the "cake" part, and the book learning is the frosting. **In other words, focus on the relationships and the book learning will come.**

This simple thought keeps me sane on those days when we must take a break (again) because of bad attitudes. I remember that **it's better for me to help my children discover a happy heart than to force the learning and hurt my relationship with them.**

9. Develop and maintain household systems that work for you.

We briefly talked about this in a previous chapter, but find a way to streamline the daily and weekly household tasks so that you can establish a sense of calm and order. Some of our family's favorite systems include monthly meal planning, freezer and crock pot meals, regular cleaning tasks such as a daily pickup of high-traffic areas, and a weekly laundry day. The main point, however, is to find a system that works for you, and to not be afraid to alter it as your family's needs change and grow.

10. Take it slowly, one step at a time.

Change comes slowly and not in smooth increments. When you're just starting back to the school year rhythm, take small bites out of the goal (instead of shoving the whole thing in).

Maybe plan to concentrate on one small change for the first few months, and see how it goes from there. Remember, it's better to have made small, permanent strides than to have made a giant leap forward (and a giant fall right back).

Most of all, look toward establishing a long-term homeschooling rhythm that works for your family.

In the past, I've found that these perspectives kept me grounded when I was lost mentally in that beautiful but-probably-not-gonna-happen idyllic homeschooling planning world.

And now, with these mindsets in place, I feel like I can dream and plan—in a much healthier way.

Points to Ponder

• Which mindsets for helpful back to school planning mentioned above was the most innovative for you? Which ones do you plan to implement this year?

For Additional Info

• The Ultimate Guide to Homeschool Planning: Tips and Top Resources for Scheduling Success

• Discovering and Celebrating Tiny Miracles

• Mommy Child Dates: My Favorite Way to Celebrate and Assess Our School Year

• Homeschool Sanity Savers Part 1: Monthly Meal Planning, Monthly Shopping and the Crock Pot

• How to Have Your Own Family Meal Prep Day

• How to Make Your Own Freezer Meals (16 Tips and 2 Recipes)

• Homeschool Sanity Savers Part 2: Daily and Weekly Household Routines That Work for Your Family

Helpful Resources

• Homeschool Planet online homeschool planner

• "You Are Special Today" Red Plate

• Plan to Be Flexible

• "rhythm: Guiding Your Family to Their Ideal Learning Flow" Online Video Course

Related Activities and Printables in This Book

• Back to School Checklist

PART 4:
TIME TO GET STARTED!

CHAPTER 8: TRADITIONS AND TRIALS: YOUR FIRST FEW DAYS

From cleaning out to setting up, and from establishing rhythms to creating learning plans, we've covered quite a bit of ground so far in this book! And at this point in the back to school process, **we're only a few days away from the big start date!**

To celebrate the start of a new year, many moms enjoy incorporating fun back-to-school traditions in their planning. So, in that spirit, I'm sharing our family's favorites.

OUR 6 FAVORITE BACK TO SCHOOL TRADITIONS

1. A special dinner and family game night the evening before school starts.

Set the tone for a fun school year with a special dinner (ours is always "make-your-own-pizza night") and plan a few awesome family activities together!

2. The kids complete a fun annual "back to school questionnaire."

Spend a few minutes on Pinterest and you'll find some adorable, fill-in-the-blank-type questionnaires where a child can write his favorite toy; something he loves to do,;his favorite summer memory, etc. These are priceless, wonderful little treasures that can be stored with other precious school artwork and papers.

3. Take a first-day-of-school picture with some sort of prop that tells their grade.

This has become quite popular over the last few years. Some moms create a special board or print a fun paper that tells each child's grade. The child then holds the sign in the picture, thus marking that child's first day of school in that grade.

I love that idea… but honestly, I never seem to be organized enough to print out one of those cute signs for each of the grades in our school!

So, instead, I take the non-fancy, low-tech approach. I hand each child a whiteboard and tell them to write their name and grade on the whiteboard (in a fancy design) using dry-erase pens. My only request is that they make their name and grade legible for the picture. I actually prefer doing it this way now because it also incorporates the child's artistic abilities at that age/stage into the photo.

4. Special time of prayer with my husband the night before.

The night before school starts, my husband and I talk through all aspects of the school year and any concerns we anticipate (behavioral issues, curriculum concerns, etc). Then we take some time together to pray aloud as a couple through those concerns.

5. Special celebration at the end of the first week (no matter how rough it was!)

At the end of our first official week of school, I plan something *super fun* for us to do that following weekend. Whether that's going for a hike, riding bikes together, or simply making a fun dessert as a family, I try to find something that focuses on building relationships.

6. I plan a date night with my husband at the end of that first week.

Back to school is a culmination of weeks and sometimes months of hard work. And yet, at the same time, it's also a beginning of a new learning chapter for the family. I believe that both are a cause for celebration! So we try to make time to go out and get alone together.

Would you like more inspiration from other moms? I put together an Ultimate List of Back to School Traditions here.

A SLOW EASING INTO SCHOOL

Last week, we've had several idyllic blue-sky days, with lots of puffy clouds and a gentle breeze.

But this week, the weather was scorching-hot: the kind of sticky misery that keeps one inside with the air-conditioning on.

Which doesn't quite make sense since we're supposed to be getting cooler instead of warmer as fall nears, right?

I'm sure you have something similar happening in your neck of the woods. As the days tick by, none of us know the exact weather pattern from now through fall, but we know that *eventually* our days will downshift into cooler temps and there will be no doubt that fall has arrived.

I mention these slow back-and-forth shifts in weather patterns because I love how our homeschooling can parallel this beautifully natural flow between seasons.

During the last few weeks of summer, I find us slowly beginning the process of starting our typical school rhythm.

Not that I even mention the word "school," mind you: **I just kind of start encouraging the kids toward learning projects and activities.**

These days are an unpredictable blend of outside exploration, and the beginning of some (very loose) traditional school learning. I may introduce a reading curriculum back in for the younger kids. Or perhaps we start playing some math learning card games together. Just like the cooler days of autumn eventually come, our school days eventually flow into more structured learning and less time for play.

And as our official "first day of school" gets closer, **I purposely tighten our schedule and routine so that it won't be a huge shock for us to suddenly be out of summer mode.**

I think this seasonal ebb-and-flow is a more natural way to teach kids. It's acknowledging that, like the seasons, the learning style is changing and we're embracing it.

If we homeschoolers really do want our kids to have an exploratory-type school mindset, (instead of a "sit down because it's school time" type), **then a gradual transition back to learning is an excellent way to support it.**

ANTICIPATING A (NOT SO SMOOTH) LEARNING FLOW

I will be the first to admit that, even with the most organized classroom and learning plans (and a slow ease back into learning), **there will be some back to school drama.**

It's a big, huge, enormous shift to go back to school, and there's no getting around that.

I wish I could tell you that I have fully accepted this fact, but my nose would be growing if I did.

Every year I seem to be caught off guard by the back to school madness.

After only a few days "officially" into our school year, I often find myself upset, defeated and disgusted because all the luster has worn off my homeschool plans.

It's not that learning isn't happening or that the curriculum plans aren't a good fit. **Instead it's just a clash between the theoretical attempts at organizing the learning, and** the messy, not-always-predictable reality of teaching children.

It's similar to when we endure a hard workout for the first time after several months of inactivity. Muscles hurt and ache, and the entire experience feels like a major shock to the body!

So I've found that it's critical that I prepare myself for these big changes, and that when the changes come, that I appropriately re-frame them so that I can see them from a truth-filled perspective.

BACK TO SCHOOL: 5 EXPECTATIONS EVERY HOMESCHOOL MOM NEEDS TO ADOPT

We'll talk more about facing back-to-school fears in the final chapter of this book ("The Most Important Thing I Want to Tell You").

But first, I want to mention some expectations that we homeschoolers should adopt, especially in those first few days of school.

1. Expect grouchiness.

This is a big, enormous shift back for our kids. Seriously. There's a lot being thrown at them (and most of it brand new curriculum and ideas). So while we shouldn't allow rudeness and disrespect, I also feel that we need to give our children extra grace during this time of transition.

2. Expect the learning to take much longer than normal at first.

For several weeks now, our kids have been out of their typical school rhythm and, in addition, they may have simply forgotten certain learning skills. It's amazing what summer break can do to juvenile brains (even when summer break still includes pockets of learning!).

3. Expect each of your kids to have at least one meltdown that first week.

This kind of goes without being said after talking about the two previous expectations, right?

4. Expect *yourself* to have at least one meltdown that first week.

Uh, yeah. Just know that it's probably coming. And expect that it may involve sobbing, passionate prayers behind closed doors, and maybe even a few sessions of pounding-your-fists-into-the-bed (I know, I know… we're way too mature to do something like that. But if you *do* find yourself in this situation, just know that you have company.)

5. Expect that something in your subject plan or overall homeschooling approach will need to be adjusted.

Once the tears have subsided and you're able to get past those initial first days of back-to-school craziness, it's a good idea to take an honest look at your learning plans.

Please hear me: I'm not saying that you should automatically abandon your homeschool plans if things are difficult at first.

What I'm saying is that **there may need to be some small adjustments made, such as adding this part in or taking that part out.** These kinds of little changes are par for the course since we're always trying to be sensitive to how to best introduce learning to our children.

THREE FINAL THINGS TO REMEMBER

In addition to what we talked about above, can I mention three other mindsets that are helpful to adopt during that first week back to school?

1. Try to lighten your load in other areas, if possible.

It's probably not the best week to introduce a new sport or activity for your child. Or to give yourself a new commitment outside the home that week. I know that seems like common sense, but this can be hard to do, especially since so many things "start back up" at back to school time.

2. Plan something nice for yourself.

Girl, you just busted your tail putting all of this together! This homeschooling stuff isn't for wimps! Make sure you do something (anything!) nice for yourself during that back to school week. Even if it's just taking a relaxing bath one night. Or maybe you can treat yourself to a pedicure or a night out for coffee with friends. Determine what you would consider relaxing and enjoyable, and make it happen!

3. Take it one day at a time.

Remember, you don't have to take on all the cares and concerns of the entire school year right now. You don't even have to take on the whole back to school week at once! Just take each day one breath at a time. You can do this!

Points to Ponder

• Which of these techniques will you try this year as you do your final prep for back to school?

• What would you consider relaxing and rewarding after the first few days of school? How could you plan to treat yourself?

For Additional Info

• The Ultimate List of Back to School Traditions

• Out of School? Here's How We Fight Summer Brain Rot

• Stolen Moments: How a Stressed Mom Can Find Everyday Rest

• Homeschool Sanity Savers Part 3: 50 Practical Tools to Manage Stress and Encourage Peace

Helpful Resources

• Plan to Be Flexible

Related Activities and Printables in This Book

• Back to School Checklist

CHAPTER 9: THE MOST IMPORTANT THING I WANT TO TELL YOU

I was thinking about you yesterday, friend, and thinking about how you might be feeling about all the back to school madness. Because I know how I feel every year at this time: Overwhelmed.

Whether this fall will be your first or your fourteenth as a homeschooler, I believe the question in the back of all of our minds is:

How in the world are we going to do this?

Whether this fall will be your first or your fourteenth as a homeschooler, I believe that's a question that plagues all of us.

You see, we can make our plans. We can craft our carefully chosen schedules and line up our books neat in a row.

And yet, the reality of teaching children is that it never ever ends up as we originally thought it would.

Bottom line: We will fail, in some way, shape, or other. We will mess up. Our kids will mess up. And our homeschool year won't turn out like we expected.

I'm not saying this to trouble you, or to add more weight to your load.

I'm simply speaking the truth. I think the "how are we going to do this" question is a demon we all face at this time of year, and friend, I want you to know that you're not alone in facing it.

I also want to speak openly about this because healing comes when we can pull these thoughts out of the dank, cloudy areas of our mind and into the brilliant light of Truth.

First, let's look a little closer at why failure as a homeschooler is so terrifying, and how it can keep us from living that full, joy-filled homeschool life.

THE TRUTHS BEHIND THE PROBLEM

How *will* we teach our kids all that they need to know? How can this seemingly insurmountable task (one fraught with impossibilities and questions and miracles) possibly come to pass when we feel, many times, so ill-equipped to make it happen?

I feel you. I hear you. I go through those emotions every year, too.

You see, when our children are handed to us—either at their birth or much later on in their lives—we sense the preciousness of the gift. These are wondrous little lives who will be looking to *us* for guidance and direction.

If we consider this too deeply (and allow ourselves to awaken to the truly wretched condition of our souls) then we can become scared to death at the thought that we are now responsible for this slow guiding of a life.

And that feeling intensifies with each year that passes (*Am I doing enough?*); with each time we see ourselves fail in our parenting (*Why in the world did I do that?*) and, I believe, has the potential to elevate to its highest degree when we make the decision that, yes, we want to homeschool.

That's because we humans have this natural ability to ruminate on all the bad things we've done—all the times we've messed up and fallen short of our own expectations.

And when we decide to add the title of "homeschool mom" to our resume, all of those past mistakes and failings are eager to present themselves in a steady line. Not to mention that society (and perhaps some family members, friends and neighbors) are quick to point out all of homeschooling's impossibilities.

Some days, this added responsibility seems more than we can bear. And It's so easy to allow our minds to wallow on the times we feel we missed the mark.

The problem with parenting is that, not only are we not given a guidebook, we're not given the ability to see the ultimate culmination of our daily work. We must trust and pay attention to the nuances of character—those moments when we are able to see into the true condition of the child's developing inner man.

And those nuances aren't always readily seen.

We can find ourselves caught up in what others are doing (the latest, the greatest, the seemingly perfect) and forget that there's a reason why our own mission can only be completed by us.

These thoughts—and so many others—can bind us fast.

They can choke out both our confidence as homeschoolers and our passion for the art of homeschooling itself.

SHOWERS OF TRUTH AND PEACE

As I've been writing this (sharing my own mini-confessional as I've layed these emotions bare), I've felt slight quickenings in my spirit—revelations of truth for the miry, murky thoughts.

I know these feelings well enough. I know those quiet whispers to be His voice speaking hope to my troubled heart.

Here's what I hear Him—the author of truth, the creator of all things, and the one who holds all things together—saying to me, like a rich balm to my soul.

1. You don't have to do it on your own. I am the great "I AM" and I want to walk with you through your everyday:

I will be with you on the days when you don't know what to say to that child that just won't sit still;

I'll give you inspired teaching ideas when the teacher's guide isn't cutting it; and I'll give you endless patience when you are tired, exhausted and just want to quit.

2. You don't have to have it all figured out now. I've provided enough grace and power for you to get through each moment one at a time.

I'm not asking you to go two months, two days or even two hours into the future. Rest with me here and trust.

Believe that I will show you what to do each day, step by step.

3. You don't have to make it all happen. Remember that your richest "teaching times" come in those quiet moments of just being together with your kids.

And here's the key: You don't need to plan for those priceless teaching moments. Establish the atmosphere (and do your part to soften your attitude) but let me take care of the when and the how. Just be faithful, be available and my daughter, let me take care of the rest.

4. You will fail, even when you give your best. Expect the mistakes to come. Be ready for them and not surprised by them. I am able to work more perfectly within those "mistakes" because that is when my spirit can shine through you to show redemption. I don't expect you to do this job perfectly, so you shouldn't either.

And lastly, he's telling me (and you):

5. You may fail, but your failures don't define who you are. Nothing can change the way I feel about you and your kids. Nothing you do can take you or them from my grasp. I am bigger than your failures, and in my own incomprehensible way, I can use those failures to bring a beauty greater than you could have ever expected. I can use those failures to show you and your kids that your homeschool journey doesn't have to be perfect to be good.

FROM ONE FLAWED MOM TO ANOTHER

My friends, be encouraged, be blessed and be willing to welcome the entirety of the homeschool experience (which means, sometimes, facing fears about our own failures).

If you've homeschooled in the past, consider what in previous homeschool years made you feel like a failure. And for this year, ask yourself: **What am I most afraid of?** What is the worst thing that could happen this year in my homeschool? And how will I feel if it will happen? Will I still be accepted and loved if it happens (the answer is yes)? Will I have messed this whole homeschooling thing up (the answer is no)?

This year, don't let failure hold you back from living the fullest life possible.

Go ahead and create your plans. Write down your goals and outlines for the year.

And then release your grip on it, allowing God to work out His bright and beautiful plan in the midst of your imperfect homeschool.

It will all turn out differently than we think it will... but it will still be magnificent.

Let these truths empower and encourage you as you begin your new homeschool year!

I am thrilled for you and excited to see what you will discover!

Points to Ponder

• What overwhelms you the most about this school year? What are you most afraid of?

• Which of these thoughts brings you the most comfort, and what can you do to remind yourself of them in the everyday chaos of homeschooling?

For Additional Info

• When Homeschooling Is Lonely and Hard: An Honest Conversation from One Homeschool Mom to Another

• 18 Verses on Homeschooling Joy

• Mom Competition: Can We Stop the Madness?

• This Magic Moment: Thoughts on Enjoying and Fully Living This Homeschool Journey

• Turning the Tables: When a Child Brings You Comfort

• The Fine Art of Homeschooling: Homeschooling Lessons from the Master Artist

Helpful Resources

• "Focusing on Progress…Not Perfection" Printable

Related Activities and Printables in This Book

• Back to School Checklist

INDEX: ACTIVITIES AND PRINTABLES

This section contains the charts, journaling prompts and other tools referenced throughout the book. These reproducible tools are designed to make your back-to-school planning easy and streamlined from year-to-year.

- **Back to School Checklist**

- **Developing Your "Why" Journaling Prompts**

- **Taking Inventory Charts: What Do You Have and What Do You Need?**

  - General School Supply Needs

  - School Needs by Subject

  - List of Needs for Entire Homeschool

  - List of Needs for Co-Op or Other Teaching

- **"Pillars and Boundaries" and "Goals with Grace" Worksheets**

  - Pillars and Boundaries Worksheet

  - Goals with Grace Worksheet

- **The Learning Resource Grid**

  - Learning Resource Grid

- **Reading Grids**

  - Family Read Aloud Reading List Chart

  - Grade Level Reading List Chart (Fiction)

  - Grade Level Reading List Chart (Non-Fiction)

- **Subject Plan Worksheet**
  - Subject Plan
- **Other Helpful Resources**
  - My Memory Box
  - The Dollar Store Back to School Supplies Shopping List
  - Plan to Be Flexible (plus exclusive coupon codes)

NOTE: If you would like a digital version of these files, simply go to the "Back to School Survival Manual: Additional Resources and Information" page to download the files.

BACK TO SCHOOL CHECKLIST

STEP 1: Prepare myself mentally: How will I handle the outside influences? What is my overall confidence level regarding this school year?

Helpful Resources

- Chapter 1: Mama, This Is Your School (and No One Else's)!
- Needs and Opinions Chart

STEP 2: Develop my family's homeschool "why" and customize it to this year's needs.

Helpful Resources

- Chapter 2: Why Are You Doing This, Anyway?
- Developing Your Why Journaling Prompts

STEP 3: Clean out and organize my homeschool area.

Helpful Resources

- Chapter 3: Conquering the Chaos and Clutter
- My Memory Box: Kids School Paper Organizer

STEP 4: Set up a master school year calendar.

Helpful Resources

- Plan to Be Flexible

STEP 5: Take inventory of our school supplies and determine curriculum needs.

Helpful Resources

- Chapter 4: What Do You Have and What Do You Need?
- Taking Inventory Charts

STEP 6: Restock our school supplies and purchase curriculum.

Helpful Resources

- Chapter 4: What Do You Have and What Do You Need?
- Taking Inventory Charts
- Dollar Store Back to School Supplies Shopping List (buy it here)

STEP 7: Set up our learning space.

STEP 8: Establish our overall family rhythm for this season.

STEP 9: Gather learning resources and create learning lists and subject plans.

Helpful Resources

- Learning Resource Grid
- Grade-Level Reading List Charts (Fiction, Non-Fiction and Family Read-Aloud)

STEP 10: Plan any back-to-school traditions.

STEP 11: Relax and slowly integrate back into the school rhythm.

STEP 12: Throughout the Year: Offer myself (and the kids) grace as our learning rhythm changes

DEVELOPING YOUR "WHY" JOURNALING PROMPTS

My guess is that if you have made the decision to homeschool, you've probably thought through (at least partially) the "whys" behind the decision. But have you worked through the "why nots"?

Note: I will be playing devil's advocate here in some of these questions to help you dig out any of those potential fears. I've tried to bring up common objections to the homeschooling lifestyle (that many are quick to share their opinion on) so that you can think through your response and be confident and peace-filled in your answer.

Remember: Do not be afraid of the hidden questions or fears you may have! By bringing those to light here and addressing them, you can gather more information, seek wise council and build a solid foundation for your "why."

Why do you feel that homeschooling is the best option for your family in this season? List your reasons.

    Educational reasons:

    Emotional/relational reasons:

    Spiritual reasons:

    Other reasons:

How will (or how does) homeschooling help your overall family relationship?

How will (or how does) homeschooling intensify family relationships or bring out sibling or parent/child challenges?

How will you manage the additional stress of "being with your children all day"?

How will (or how does) homeschooling affect each of your individual children and their personalities or unique learning abilities?

Positive ways it will affect each child:

Challenges each child may face as homeschoolers:

Do you have any concerns about being "able" to teach your children? Do you feel equipped and up to the task? Do you feel that you need additional education (formal or informal) to teach your child?

As a homeschooler, how do you plan to maintain your other responsibilities, such as managing the family's overall rhythms, keeping a home, and taking care of other smaller, non-school-aged children?

How do you plan to provide social time with other children, and how much time (on average per week) do you feel is adequate for each of your kids?

If you have multiple children, how do you plan to manage all of their learning needs, especially if your children have large gaps between ages?

How will you teach those subjects that were a challenge for you in school?

How will you keep records and maintain state standards?

How will you know what to teach your kids for each grade level?

What do you most like (or do you look forward to most) as a home-schooler?

What are you most afraid of as a homeschooler?

What is your children's response (or what do you anticipate their response to be) to the idea of learning at home?

Will you follow a more planned learning approach; allow children to explore on their own; or provide a learning environment that is a combination of both?

How will you handle it when your children don't want to do school or are otherwise being difficult?

What is the number one reason why you want to homeschool?

Final overall thoughts:

TAKING INVENTORY CHARTS: WHAT DO YOU HAVE AND WHAT DO YOU NEED?

There are three types of charts in this school supplies inventory: individual child charts; entire homeschool charts; and charts for co-op or other extra teaching needs.

Individual Child Charts

Because we each school differently (and some subjects may require a range of books and supplies), I've created a few different templates that will work when determining each child's needs (and how your current supplies might meet those needs). Each document contains a column where you can make a plan on how to get that particular supply (if it is needed).

I've also filled in some subject names in the "subject" column in the charts. Again, I've tried to include as many subjects as possible. With this in mind, you may find that a child is going to use all or some of the subjects listed here. If you're not planning to teach a particular subject listed, simply cross it off the chart. There are also blank spaces in some versions of the charts so that you can add in subjects not listed here or customize the lists. In short, customize these charts to work for you!

Here are four charts for gathering school supply needs for each individual child:

- Individual Child: general school supplies needs
- Individual Child: list of all subjects on one page and their needs
- Individual Child: blank list with room for all subjects on one page and their needs
- Individual Child: blank list of seven subjects on one page and their needs

Entire Homeschool and Co-Op or Other Teaching Needs Charts:

I've created a chart for gathering supplies for your entire homeschool, and a chart to address supply needs for a co-op where you may teach.

• Entire Homeschool: List of needs for the entire school

• For Co-Op or Other Teaching Needs: List of possible needs

Don't forget to review your electronic resources (digital curriculum or books on your hard drive, for example) as part of your assessment and inventory.

Happy organizing!

Child's Name: _____

Grade: _____ **School Year:** _____

GENERAL SCHOOL SUPPLY NEEDS

Subject	Curriculum/Books On Hand	Curriculum/Books to Buy	Action Plan

Child's Name: _____

Grade: _____ **School Year:** _____

GENERAL SCHOOL SUPPLY NEEDS

BACKPACK? LAPTOP? DESK? ORGANIZATION SYSTEM? ETC.

Child's Name: _____

Grade: _____   **School Year:** _____

SCHOOL NEEDS BY SUBJECT

Subject	Curriculum/Books On Hand	Curriculum/Books to Buy	Action Plan

Child's Name: _____

Grade: _____   **School Year:** _____

SCHOOL NEEDS BY SUBJECT

Subject	Curriculum/Books On Hand	Curriculum/Books to Buy	Action Plan
Bible			
Character Training			
Math			
Phonics/Reading			
Spelling			
Writing			
Handwriting			
Copywork			
Nature Study			

Child's Name: _____

Grade: _____ **School Year:** _____

SCHOOL NEEDS BY SUBJECT

Subject	Curriculum/Books On Hand	Curriculum/Books to Buy	Action Plan
Art			
Music			
History			
Geography			
Literature			
Philosophy			
Government			
Journaling			
Science			

LIST OF NEEDS FOR ENTIRE HOMESCHOOL

Item Type	Example Items	Items to Buy	Action Plan
Paper Products	lined paper, notebooks		
Paper Supply Holders	folders, 3-ring binders		
Classroom Supplies	glue sticks, paper clips		
Writing Tools & Storage	pens, pencils, pencil holders		
School Project Supplies	posterboard, foamcore		
Teaching Tools	dry erase board and pens		
Motivation/ Encouragement	stickers, reward charts		
Helpful Books			

LIST OF NEEDS FOR ENTIRE HOMESCHOOL

Item Type	Example Items	Items to Buy	Action Plan
Electronic Accessories			
Specialty Items			
Toddler Busy Activities			
General Learning Play Activities			
Rewards (& "Getting Out the Wiggles" Activities)			
Art & Craft Supplies			
Field Trip/Co-Op Supplies			

LIST OF NEEDS FOR CO-OP OR OTHER TEACHING

Item Type	Example Items	Items to Buy	Action Plan
Paper Products	lined paper, notebooks		
Paper Supply Holders	folders, 3-ring binders		
Classroom Supplies	glue sticks, paper clips		
Writing Tools & Storage	pens, pencils, pencil holders		
School Project Supplies	posterboard, foamcore		
Teaching Tools	dry erase board and pens		
Motivation/ Encouragement	stickers, reward charts		

"PILLARS AND BOUNDARIES" AND "GOALS WITH GRACE" WORKSHEETS

Pillars with Boundaries and Goals with Grace are the key concepts that serve as the science behind homeschool rhythms. They are the starting point for determining how we can guide our children's individual learning rhythms.

This section includes three separate worksheets:

1. Pillars and Boundaries Worksheet Step 1: Establish Foundational Pillars

2. Pillars and Boundaries Worksheet Step 2: Build Support Beams

3. Goals with Grace Worksheet

In order to best explain how to use these charts, I'd like to give a quick review of the definitions for pillars and boundaries (the first two critical elements of a homeschool rhythm).

Pillars are simply key, habitual practices that frame the contents of our days. Pillars provide a sense of order and structure without the rigidity of a schedule. Defining daily pillars is the first step in creating a rhythm. Pillars can include regular, occurring activities such as "sleeping/waking" times, "meals" and "rest time." These pillars are set at approximate times (for example, breakfast is at 8:00 a.m. and lunch is at 12:00 p.m.) and the learning flows around them.

Boundaries are those practices we establish to keep pillars strong. We need these mental attitudes (specific thought patterns we will begin to adapt) and tangible activities (actual tasks we will or will not do) as general supports to reinforce the pillars. This is where the idea of pillars goes from being merely theoretical to the actual.

The second two critical aspects of a homeschool rhythm are "goals" and "grace."

Goals are those long or short term plans that we make. Goals are the guiding factors of our homeschool—the what we will attempt do in our days. They're the target that we shoot for.

However, goals can sometimes have a flip side: goals can be lofty, idealistic concepts that exist solely on paper (which renders them meaningless); or goals can make us feel guilty (a list of ways that we're not measuring up). Goals are incredibly powerful for helping us shape our destinies, but we have to hold them with an open hand that allows for the realities of life to happen.

Grace is the ability to forgive imperfection and to allow "real life" to happen. Grace allows us to give ourselves space and permission for the goals or plans we've made to not turn out perfectly.

PILLARS AND BOUNDARIES WORKSHEET

Step 1: Establish Foundational Pillars

What pillars do you currently have in place in your homeschooling days? Do you need to add any additional pillars to bring more of a sense of order? How are these pillars arranged in the day (or how do you plan to arrange them)? If they are already in place, are you happy with how they are arranged in the day? This first chart will help us answer these questions (I've filled in some "typical" pillars, but I've added a blank pillar row so that you can add more if you'd like). Don't get hung up on boundaries yet. Step 2 (the next chart) will help us figure that out.

Daily Pillar #1	Boundaries: Mental Attitudes	Boundaries: Tangible Activities	Baby Steps to Implementation
Sleeping/Waking			
Daily Pillar #2	Boundaries: Mental Attitudes	Boundaries: Tangible Activities	Baby Steps to Implementation
Meals/Eating			
Daily Pillar #3	Boundaries: Mental Attitudes	Boundaries: Tangible Activities	Baby Steps to Implementation
Rest/Down-Time			
Daily Pillar #4	Boundaries: Mental Attitudes	Boundaries: Tangible Activities	Baby Steps to Implementation

Step 2: Build Support Beams

Now that we've identified the pillars for your home, we're going to determine the boundaries (specific mental attitudes and tangible activities) that can serve as support beams to these pillars. We'll also determine what baby steps need to happen to establish these boundaries.

Daily Pillar #1	Approximate Times/ Placement in the Day	Happy with Placement? Small Changes to be Made?
Sleeping/Waking		
Daily Pillar #2	Approximate Times/ Placement in the Day	Happy with Placement? Small Changes to be Made?
Meals/Eating		
Daily Pillar #3	Approximate Times/ Placement in the Day	Happy with Placement? Small Changes to be Made?
Rest/Down-Time		
Daily Pillar #4	Approximate Times/ Placement in the Day	Happy with Placement? Small Changes to be Made?

GOALS WITH GRACE WORKSHEET

Keeping in mind that no goals can ever be perfectly attained, this worksheet allows us to identify specific attitudes to have or actions to take that can help us keep an attitude of grace while pursuing these goals.

A few definitions for the chart below:

"Supports": What practices can I build into my life to accomplish/maintain this specific grace-filled attitude/action?

"Removal": What lies or habitual thought patterns/issues need to be addressed and removed in order for me to accomplish/maintain this specific grace-filled attitude action?

"Baby Steps": What are some small, tangible shifts that I can make right now to begin to move in the direction I ultimately want to go?

Grace-Filled Attitude or Action	Supports	Removal	Baby Steps
#1.			
#2.			
#3.			
#4.			

THE LEARNING RESOURCE GRID

The **Learning Resource Grid** is an amazing tool. You can gather all the potential learning materials for a particular subject! This may include textbooks and "official" curriculum but it also includes resources from online places.

The grid is divided into each of these types of learning resources:

- Core Text
- Supplemental Books or Texts
- Worksheets/Notebooks
- Websites/Online games
- Crafts, Experiments, Games, Other Hands-On Activities
- Videos or Audio Books

Why is **The Learning Resource Grid** so powerful? Because it is the "buffet" of resources and ideas from which you can gather each week. Let this document house all your great potential learning adventures!

Feel free to copy or print one for each subject!

LEARNING RESOURCE GRID

Core Text(s)	Supplemental Books or Texts (Read Aloud or Independent)	Worksheets/ Notebooks	Websites/ Online Games	Crafts, Experiments, Games, Other Hands-on Activities	Videos or Audio Books

READING GRIDS

Have you ever (happily) run across a great list of books that's appropriate for your child's age/grade? There seems to be a plethora of them on Pinterest. These are great... except that it can be nearly impossible to gather all of these books together into a compilation list that works for your individual student.

That's where these Reading Grids come in! Divided into three different categories or book styles, these grids are an excellent repository for creating your own customized lists for your family!

There are three Reading Grids in this section:

1. Family Read Aloud Reading List Chart

2. Grade Level Reading List Chart (Fiction)

3. Grade Level Reading List Chart (Non-Fiction)

Feel free to copy or print one for each child!

FAMILY READ ALOUD READING LIST CHART

Title/Author	Classic or For Fun?	Where to Find	Comments	Read?

GRADE LEVEL READING LIST CHART (FICTION)

Title/Author	Classic or For Fun?	Where to Find	Comments	Read?

GRADE LEVEL READING LIST CHART (NON-FICTION)

Title/Author	Classic or For Fun?	Where to Find	Comments	Read?

SUBJECT PLAN WORKSHEET

Once you've gathered all the potential resources and activities for a subject (or books for a child to read), now it's time to formulate a rough plan for the type of learning activities that can actually happen.

This is the purpose for the **Subject Plan Worksheet**. On this worksheet, you will give an approximation of the learning activities for each student during that given period. Again, there's still flexibility here (and we're not assigning these to an hour-by-hour schedule) but we're making a list of goals to complete for this student in these subjects during a specific time period.

Again, feel free to copy this worksheet to accommodate as many weeks as you need (although I would not recommend planning more than four to six weeks at a time).

SUBJECT PLAN

For: _____

I suggest only planning four to six weeks out in advance so that you can keep your school rhythm flexible.

Date	Topic	Activities for Week	Resources Required	Comments

OTHER HELPFUL RESOURCES

My Memory Box: Kids' School Paper Organizing System

Not sure what to do with your children's special school papers, priceless artwork and valuable awards/certificates?

With the My Memory Box organizing system, I systematically store each of those precious treasures–safely and efficiently–for my kids… and you can too!

Conquer that ever-mounting stack of your child's precious artwork and special school papers in a stylish, fun and effective way!

Get this printable to assemble your own My Memory Box: Kids' School Paper Organizing System!

Dollar Store Back to School Supplies Shopping List

This invaluable, seven-page, full-color printable contains a four-page shopping list that categorizes all your necessary back-to-school items—all found at the Dollar Store!

There are 191 items are grouped into the following 14 categories for shopping ease.

Grab the Dollar Store Back to School Supplies Shopping List today and make back to school supply shopping super easy and cheap!

Visit the
"Back to School Survival Manual: Additional Information and Resources" page on VibrantHomeschooling.com
for **product coupon codes exclusively for Back to School Survival Manual readers!**

Plan to Be Flexible

This powerful book (available as a print or e-book) describes "rhythm-based home-schooling"—a natural, realistic approach for guiding curriculum planning and the daily flow of homeschooling life.

You will:

- Analyze what's working (and what's not) in your homeschool.

- Develop a flexible and goal-oriented curriculum plan for each student.

- Discover why rhythms (not schedules) are the secret to homeschooling sanity.

- Learn how to homeschool with joy and freedom

Made in the USA
Las Vegas, NV
02 September 2022

54578452R00072